DRUGS
The Straight Facts

Ecstasy

DRUGS The Straight Facts

DRUGS
The Straight Facts

Ecstasy

Brock E. Schroeder

Consulting Editor
David J. Triggle
University Professor
School of Pharmacy and Pharmaceutical Sciences
State University of New York at Buffalo

CHELSEA HOUSE
PUBLISHERS
A Haights Cross Communications Company
Philadelphia

CHELSEA HOUSE PUBLISHERS

VP, NEW PRODUCT DEVELOPMENT Sally Cheney
DIRECTOR OF PRODUCTION Kim Shinners
CREATIVE MANAGER Takeshi Takahashi
MANUFACTURING MANAGER Diann Grasse

Staff for ECSTASY

ASSOCIATE EDITOR Beth Reger
PRODUCTION EDITOR Megan Emery
PHOTO EDITOR Sarah Bloom
SERIES & COVER DESIGNER Terry Mallon
LAYOUT 21st Century Publishing and Communications, Inc.

A Haights Cross Communications ⚓ Company

http://www.chelseahouse.com

First Printing

1 3 5 7 9 8 6 4 2

Library of Congress Cataloging-in-Publication Data

Schroeder, Brock E.
    Ecstasy/Brock E. Schroeder.
        p. cm. — (Drugs, the straight facts)
Includes bibliographical references and index.
Contents: The history of ecstasy—The neurobiology of ecstasy use—Ecstasy's
long term effects—Other serious health effects—Teenage trends and attitudes—
The fight against MDMA smugglers—Treatment and prevention.
    ISBN 0-7910-7633-4
    1. Ecstasy (Drug)—Juvenile literature. [1. Ecstasy (Drug) 2. Drug abuse.]
I. Title. II. Series.
RM666.M35S37 2003
615'.7883—dc22

                                                                    2003016565

Table of Contents

The Use and Abuse of Drugs

The issues associated with drug use and abuse in contemporary society are vexing subjects, fraught with political agendas and ideals that often obscure essential information that teens need to know to have intelligent discussions about how to best deal with the problems associated with drug use and abuse. *Drugs: The Straight Facts* aims to provide this essential information through straightforward explanations of how an individual drug or group of drugs works in both therapeutic and non-therapeutic conditions; with historical information about the use and abuse of specific drugs; with discussion of drug policies in the United States; and with an ample list of further reading.

From the start, the series uses the word *"drug"* to describe psychoactive substances that are used for medicinal or non-medicinal purposes. Included in this broad category are substances that are legal or illegal. It is worth noting that humans have used many of these substances for hundreds, if not thousands of years. For example, traces of marijuana and cocaine have been found in Egyptian mummies; the use of peyote and Amanita fungi has long been a component of religious ceremonies worldwide; and alcohol production and consumption have been an integral part of many human cultures' social and religious ceremonies. One can speculate about why early human societies chose to use such drugs. Perhaps, anything that could provide relief from the harshness of life—anything that could make the poor conditions and fatigue associated with hard work easier to bear—was considered a welcome tonic. Life was likely to be, according to the seventeenth century English philosopher Thomas Hobbes, *"poor, nasty, brutish and short."* One can also speculate about modern human societies' continued use and abuse of drugs. Whatever the reasons, the consequences of sustained drug use are not insignificant—addiction, overdose, incarceration, and drug wars—and must be dealt with by an informed citizenry.

The problem that faces our society today is how to break

the connection between our demand for drugs and the willingness of largely outside countries to supply this highly profitable trade. This is the same problem we have faced since narcotics and cocaine were outlawed by the Harrison Narcotic Act of 1914, and we have yet to defeat it despite current expenditures of approximately $20 billion per year on "the war on drugs." The first step in meeting any challenge is always an intelligent and informed citizenry. The purpose of this series is to educate our readers so that they can make informed decisions about issues related to drugs and drug abuse.

SUGGESTED ADDITIONAL READING

David T. Courtwright, *Forces of Habit. Drugs and the making of the modern world.* Cambridge, Mass.: Harvard University Press, 2001. David Courtwright is Professor of History at the University of North Florida.

Richard Davenport-Hines, *The Pursuit of Oblivion. A global history of narcotics.* New York: Norton, 2002. The author is a professional historian and a member of the Royal Historical Society.

Aldous Huxley, *Brave New World.* New York: Harper & Row, 1932. Huxley's book, written in 1932, paints a picture of a cloned society devoted to the pursuit only of happiness.

David J. Triggle, Ph.D.
University Professor
School of Pharmacy and Pharmaceutical Sciences
State University of New York at Buffalo

1

The History of Ecstasy

"This is the greatest feeling ever. I have no problems."

—Dayna, recovering Ecstasy addict,
on her first experience with Ecstasy [1]

"MDMA (ecstasy) damages brain cells, (it) is not a benign drug."

—Glen R. Hanson, acting director of the
National Institute on Drug Abuse, 2002 [2]

WHAT IS ECSTASY?

In 1912 the German pharmaceutical company Merck first synthesized and patented a compound called 3,4-methylenedioxymethamphetamine, or MDMA for short. At the time, many new chemicals were synthesized in the hopes that they might be useful in future research. MDMA, as an amphetamine-derivative, had potential as a diet drug. However, like many other compounds, research on MDMA was soon abandoned by Merck. Many pharmaceutical companies at that time applied for and received patents on everything they synthesized, just in case the compound was ever found to be useful or in case they ever decided to do more research on the compound. Many of these chemical products, like MDMA, did not show enough promise to be investigated further, and thus research was abandoned.

More than 50 years later, an American scientist named Alexander Shulgin resynthesized the compound and began experimenting with it. Shulgin believed that MDMA would be useful medically, perhaps

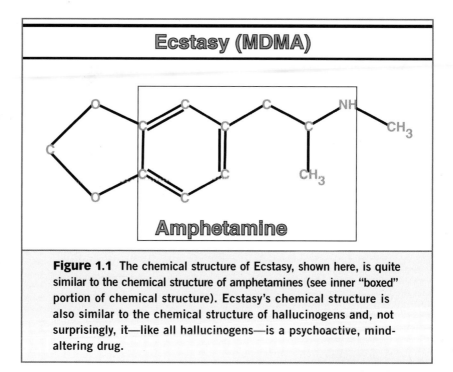

Ecstasy (MDMA)

Amphetamine

Figure 1.1 The chemical structure of Ecstasy, shown here, is quite similar to the chemical structure of amphetamines (see inner "boxed" portion of chemical structure). Ecstasy's chemical structure is also similar to the chemical structure of hallucinogens and, not surprisingly, it—like all hallucinogens—is a psychoactive, mind-altering drug.

in treating people for psychological disorders. (As will be discussed in Chapter 4, many current researchers do not believe that MDMA has useful medicinal benefits, especially when weighed against the harm that it is thought to cause.) Shortly after, in the early 1980s, MDMA (soon to be known worldwide as "Ecstasy") was just beginning to be used as a recreational drug. Ecstasy was actually named by an enterprising drug dealer, who was seeking to capitalize on this new drug. MDMA was first called "empathy" which describes its effects more appropriately as feelings of closeness, but "ecstasy" was a much more marketable name. Thus Ecstasy was born. In schools, at parties, and at a new type of function called a "rave," Ecstasy use began appearing and increasing in popularity. In the past 20 years, that simple compound, MDMA, has grown into one of the most commonly abused drugs by teenagers in America and around the world.

MDMA's chemical structure has properties that are similar to both amphetamines and hallucinogens (Figure 1.1). These chemical similarities are directly responsible for the psychoactive, mind-altering effects of the drug. Amphetamines are psychostimulants, which means they cause a "rush" or "high," increased energy, and wakefulness. In structure (and in name), MDMA is actually most similar to methamphetamine, or "speed." MDMA also has similarities with psychedelic or hallucinogenic drugs such as LSD and mescaline. While it does not usually cause overt hallucinations like LSD, the psychedelic properties of Ecstasy do cause altered perceptions and feelings of peacefulness, empathy, and acceptance.

Most often MDMA is taken in the form of a tablet (Figure 1.2), which is easily produced in illegal laboratories. Like many illegal drugs, one of the dangers of taking Ecstasy is that a user is never really sure what he or she is getting. Furthermore, it is difficult to determine the purity of a pill. From a chemical perspective, Ecstasy is relatively easy and cheap to produce. While a single tablet may only cost pennies to produce, it is sold for between $20 and $50 per pill—a hefty profit. Because of its profitability, the Ecstasy trade has become a huge industry, reaching across the entire globe. The global market is very complex. For example, a single pill might make its way from an illegal laboratory in the Netherlands to a crime syndicate in Israel, where it then may be smuggled in a plastic bag (which someone swallows and later "recovers") through customs. That pill may find its way through several dealers and middlemen before ending up at the local rave.

RAVE CULTURE

Over the past 10–15 years, the use of Ecstasy has become synonymous with all-night rave parties. Raves are well known for their high-energy techno music and nonstop dancing (Figure 1.3). Rave parties are usually held in large warehouse-like

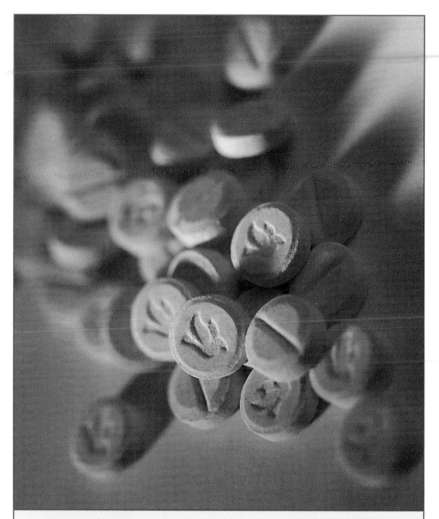

Figure 1.2 Ecstasy tablets come in many shapes and sizes, like the ones shown here. The tablets may be stamped with a variety of shapes, letters, and logos, which often make them more appealing to young and unsuspecting users.

buildings. They are often extremely crowded, and generally last well into the following morning. The mix of teenagers, dancing, and music could be an exciting and clean experience, if not for the increasing popularity of Ecstasy. Unfortunately,

Figure 1.3 Raves are known for their techno music and crowded dancing. Raves often take place in large warehouse-like buildings. While initially only popular in cities like New York and Los Angeles, raves have become common throughout the country.

the surging popularity of rave culture and Ecstasy use are not coincidental. Ecstasy not only gives people a sense of well being, but also delivers a strong burst of energy, so that a person can dance for hours at a time. Unfortunately, Ecstasy's effects do not end there. As we shall see in the following chapters, the harmful effects caused by this drug vastly outweigh the short-term excitement that the drug delivers.

Rave culture and Ecstasy use have built on each other in creating a public health epidemic. It is impossible to accurately

HANNAH'S STORY:

Hannah had definitely never been to a party like *this* before. This was amazing! All around her everything was so alive, pulsing—the techno music, the strobe lights, the people. There were red and blue and green stage lights atop the DJ's box, searching around the room, alternately catching glimpses of one person after another, dancing, happy. She had no clue who any of these people were. She only knew the one friend she came with, Amanda. So it was kind of intimidating, feeling a little lost in the crowd, but Hannah was sure that she and Amanda would have a good time together. Why in the world had she held out so long on going to raves?

As Hannah and her friend made their way further inside, Amanda stopped to talk to some guy, leaving Hannah alone. Did she know that guy? It wasn't somebody from school. Hannah decided just to hang out and wait for Amanda before going out on the floor to dance. This didn't seem like the kind of place where she wanted to dance with a bunch of strangers.

A couple minutes later, Amanda and the guy walked over to Hannah to join her. Amanda was acting weird, detached. The guy nodded his head at Hannah, gave her a slick smirk, and pulled a little plastic bag out of his pocket. Little white pills. Who is this guy and what are those?, she thought. And what's up with Amanda? The guy asked her if she wanted one of the pills, told her that her friend said she might be interested in having a good time, too. Amanda smiled and nodded, as if to say that the guy was cool and Hannah should definitely take him up on his offer.

"No thanks," said Hannah. "I don't really do that stuff."

The guy said it was X. It was nothing bad. Nothing hard. He said it would just make her feel good, relaxed, happy. Amanda was down with it, he said.

"No, really, that's okay. I'm good," Hannah replied.

Nothing to be afraid of, he said. Nothing to worry about. She'd have absolutely no worries at all if she took it.

Hannah wasn't sure.

judge the influence of one upon the other, because raves and Ecstasy use have grown together into the cultural events that they are today. The psychological effects of the drug produce both a stimulant high and an overwhelming feeling of well being, fitting in well with the close-together atmosphere of raves. For this reason, Ecstasy is also called "The Hug Drug." Rave culture, in its own right, also contributes to Ecstasy use. Ecstasy dealers are often on-hand at raves, ready to sell their product to new or experienced users. Peer pressure to use Ecstasy at raves is intense. Raves also contribute to Ecstasy use at a much more fundamental level. Biochemical research has shown that certain drugs (MDMA is a good example) actually have an increased effect at higher temperatures, such as those often experienced in densely packed raves. In other words, Ecstasy actually has a more intense effect when a person's body temperature is high or when the person is in a hot environment.

COMMON NAMES FOR MDMA

Ecstasy	Herbal Bliss
Adam	Hype
X	Love Pill
E	Rave Energy
Bean	Tachas
Charity	Wafers
E-Bombs	X-pills
Four-leaf clover	XTC

BEYOND RAVE CULTURE

While raves have become increasingly popular, Ecstasy use is not limited to these events and situations. Many people report using ecstasy in small groups of friends. People are sometimes introduced to Ecstasy by a friend or a friend-of-a-friend-of-a-friend who has tried it and wants others to join. These things may happen at small parties on Saturday nights or with one or two people on a weekday afternoon. Some people only later discover the rave scene. Also contributing to the problem is the fact that Ecstasy, because it is so available these days, is perhaps even easier for teens to get than alcohol.

The Ecstasy crisis is widespread and pervasive in the city, suburbs, and even rural areas. While many drug epidemics begin—and can stay focused—in densely populated urban areas such as New York or Los Angeles, Ecstasy use is currently widespread in every state in the country. Middle and upper-class white teenagers are by far the most likely group to begin using Ecstasy. Indeed, while so much of America feels immune to the dangers of Ecstasy, living in small towns or far from rave culture, or else living a privileged life completely detached from "Street" culture, this little pill has infiltrated every facet of our society. Even while the use of other drugs of abuse has been decreasing in the past 5–10 years, Ecstasy use has continuously increased. Its medical consequences are already clear, as Emergency Room visits due to Ecstasy use are growing at an exponential pace. Whether raves are to blame for Ecstasy use, or Ecstasy bears the sole responsibility, the end result is that teenagers are increasingly likely to use Ecstasy. As scientific research is clearly revealing, *that* is an enormous public health concern.

2

The Neurobiology of Ecstasy

"Addiction is a brain disease"

—Alan Leshner, director of the
National Institute on Drug Abuse, 1997 [3]

ACUTE PSYCHOLOGICAL EFFECTS

When taken in tablet form, as it usually is, MDMA is readily absorbed into the bloodstream, enters the brain quite easily, and begins to have its effect within 20–60 minutes after ingestion. As could be inferred from its name, users of Ecstasy describe the feeling as intense and emotional. They feel energetic and confident, yet calm because of a lack of worries or problems. Sensations such as touching someone's hair may seem incredibly pleasurable, as one has heightened sensations (touch, smell, vision, taste, and hearing). While some people have strong negative reactions to MDMA, such as confusion, paranoia, and anxiety, most people report experiencing strong positive emotional feelings.

Users of ecstasy (especially at raves) often spend entire weekends without sleep—80 hours at a time—binging on the drug. They may take an Ecstasy tablet every few hours, in order to maintain their high, and may not be able to sleep because of the stimulant qualities of the drug. What follows is a very well characterized "crash," including extreme tiredness, listlessness, and depression in most people. After coming down off of an Ecstasy high, it is very common for people to have problems concentrating at school;

often they do not even make it out of bed. Very quickly, users have trouble thinking about anything other than getting more Ecstasy and breaking free of the depressing feelings. In essence, Ecstasy feeds its own use; it brings on a depression that makes people feel like they need more Ecstasy in order to free themselves from that very depression.

People also describe serious body pain during the "crash." Their whole body aches and seems to hurt. The pain is often most intense in people's jaws. Between the depression and physical aches of Ecstasy use, many people make the mistake of feeling that the only way to escape is to take more Ecstasy. Sadly, users often find themselves trying again and again, for years after, to achieve the same feeling that they got the first time they used Ecstasy. They do not realize that it is biologically impossible for them to succeed.

ACUTE BIOLOGICAL EFFECTS

Ecstasy (or any drug for that matter) affects the brain in very specific ways. Even without drugs, a person feels the way he or she does because of changes in chemical signaling in the brain. The nerve cells in the brain, which are called neurons (Figure 2.1), make contact with each other at extremely small junctions called synapses. In this space between two neurons, chemicals called neurotransmitters are released and travel from one neuron to the next. These chemical signals are responsible for changes in the way a person feels, acts, and thinks. Happy, sad, angry, ecstatic—these emotions are all made possible by changes in the amounts of neurotransmitters being released at any one time in specific regions of the brain. For example, glutamate (a neurotransmitter) is needed in a structure of the brain called the hippocampus in order for learning to take place. Another neurotransmitter, serotonin, is intimately involved in mood, memory, hunger, sex, and sleep. Serotonin is particularly important in determining emotion and mood. For example, monkeys who have low serotonin levels are

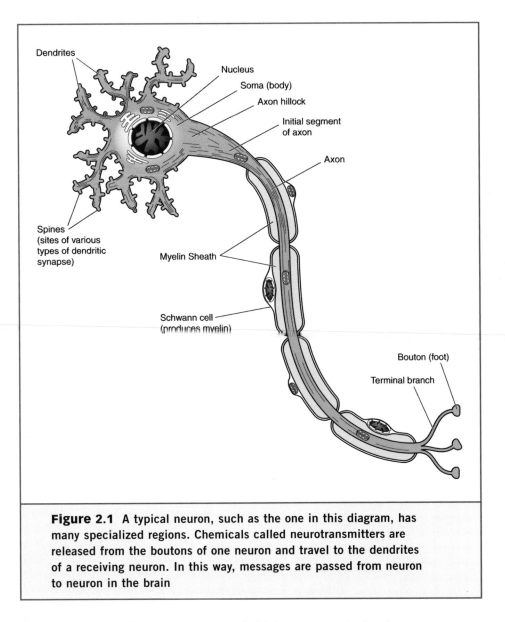

Figure 2.1 A typical neuron, such as the one in this diagram, has many specialized regions. Chemicals called neurotransmitters are released from the boutons of one neuron and travel to the dendrites of a receiving neuron. In this way, messages are passed from neuron to neuron in the brain

more aggressive than those with higher serotonin levels. Clinically depressed individuals are often prescribed anti depressant drugs such as Prozac® or Paxil®, which alleviate depression and improve mood by specifically increasing the amount of serotonin in parts of the brain. These medications help the depressed patient's serotonin levels return to normal, so that the person can function normally again.

The Up

Like Prozac and Paxil, MDMA also increases serotonin levels in the brain. The similarities end there, however. Doctor-prescribed anti-depressants are both safe and effective. Ecstasy is definitely not safe, and after the first use, becomes less safe and less effective. The primary effect of MDMA in the brain is to increase greatly the amount of serotonin in the brain's synapses (the areas in between two brain cells where signaling takes place). MDMA does this by interfering with the neurons' ability to remove serotonin from the synapse after it is released (Figure 2.2). When serotonin is released normally, under drug free conditions, it stimulates the receiving neuron and is quickly taken back up into the neuron that released it in the

HANNAH'S STORY:

All she felt was good. Hannah was so glad she had taken her friend's advice and tried X. This was the most wonderful feeling she had ever had. She was just overcome with happiness and love and energy . . . so *alive!* All around her people were dancing and singing and kissing. Absolute euphoria! Indescribable, she thought, totally indescribable. She felt like she was on the most amazingly large trampoline, jumping up so high, feet never touching the ground, flipping, spinning, soaring. She could do absolutely anything, she thought. Anything. Homework, parents, ex-boyfriend . . . who cares? This was what life is all about, she decided. Not to mention, she had met so many beautiful people there already. No doubt she'd have like ten dates for next weekend!

Feeling this way, she had no way of knowing the sadness and depression that would soon follow.

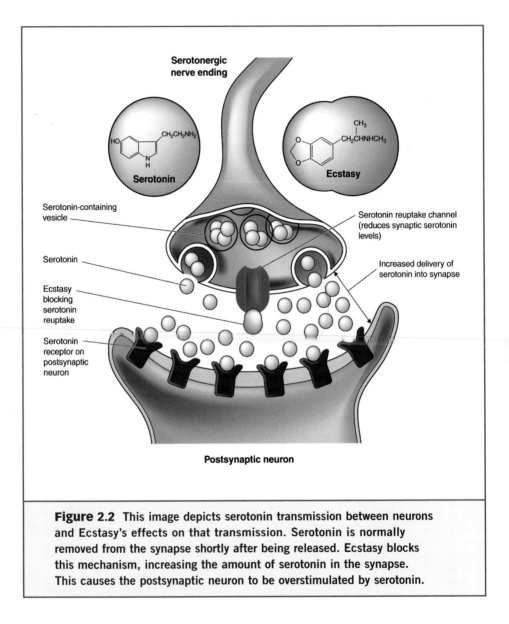

Figure 2.2 This image depicts serotonin transmission between neurons and Ecstasy's effects on that transmission. Serotonin is normally removed from the synapse shortly after being released. Ecstasy blocks this mechanism, increasing the amount of serotonin in the synapse. This causes the postsynaptic neuron to be overstimulated by serotonin.

first place. When Ecstasy is taken, serotonin builds up in the synapses, and continuously activates its target neurons. This increase in serotonin concentration is thought to be responsible for the euphoria, calmness, and loving feelings users experience. They simply have an excess of serotonin in their synapses, and that excess creates the pleasurable feelings.

MDMA also causes an increase in the concentration of the neurotransmitter dopamine. Dopamine release is involved in a number of functions in the body, including motor activity. One of its chief responsibilities, however, is to signal events that are rewarding to people, such as food or sex. When a person eats something that tastes good, his or her brain releases dopamine in very specific places. That signal is thought to identify that what the person just ate is a good thing, that he or she liked it, and that he or she should get more. The increase in dopamine release that is caused by MDMA (and which is similar to increases in dopamine caused by cocaine or amphetamine) is probably responsible for the energetic, "high" feeling. Dopamine changes are thought to be one of the key factors in the addictive nature of cocaine and amphetamine. Researchers currently believe that the dopamine signal caused by MDMA is also likely responsible for addictive properties of Ecstasy, which are discussed in more detail later in this chapter.

The serotonin system (Figure 2.3) is extremely important in a wide variety of functions in the brain. There is actually only a small percentage of neurons in the brain that release serotonin. Most of these cells reside in an area of the brain called the raphe (RAF-fay) nucleus; however, the projections of these neurons cover most of the brain, including the hippocampus, hypothalamus, and cerebral cortex. These widespread projections explain why MDMA can have effects on so many feelings and behaviors. In everyday life, a person never has a change in serotonin release in every part of the brain at the same time. When taking Ecstasy, however, there is an artificial release of serotonin everywhere. This brings about the huge number of psychological and behavioral changes that accompany Ecstasy use. For example, the hippocampus is a structure that is intricately involved in

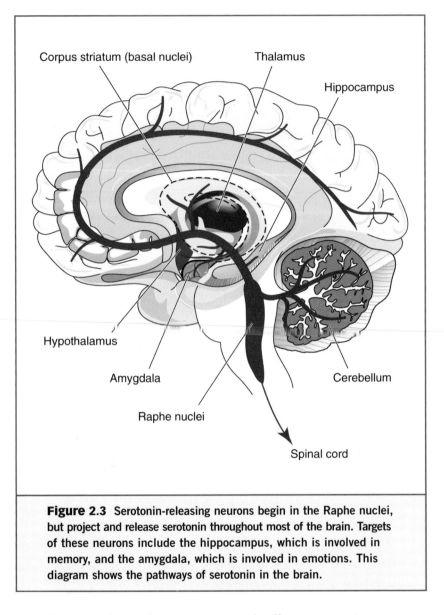

Figure 2.3 Serotonin-releasing neurons begin in the Raphe nuclei, but project and release serotonin throughout most of the brain. Targets of these neurons include the hippocampus, which is involved in memory, and the amygdala, which is involved in emotions. This diagram shows the pathways of serotonin in the brain.

both emotion and memory. Ecstasy's effects on emotion are abundantly clear, but it also has strong effects on memory (which will be discussed in some detail later). The hypothalamus is in charge of a large number of regulatory processes

HANNAH'S STORY:

It had been weeks since Hannah's first rave . . . weeks since her first experience with X. She wasn't really hanging out with Amanda anymore, either. Hannah had seen her around at a few places since then, but they just hung in different circles now.

It was Monday and school just wasn't going to happen. Not today. She was sick—that's what she told her mom. Wasn't it obvious? She was sick. She'd been sick a lot lately, though. School had become kind of optional for her. It's not that she thought school was so bad, it's just that it seemed kind of pointless. Plus, she just didn't feel well. Her legs hurt, her jaw hurt, her head hurt. This sucks, she thought. And to make matters worse, Hannah's mom was increasingly annoying her. If it wasn't one thing, it was another—school, dinner, allowance, everything. If her mom didn't get off her case, Hannah swore she was going to go insane.

The weekdays were excruciating. All Hannah could do was either lie around feeling awful, argue with her mom, or lie to her teachers. She just didn't understand why her life was so pathetic lately. But she didn't even care *why* really. She just couldn't stand it. So she hadn't been to school much in the past few weeks, so what? She didn't feel well. And all those ridiculous interrogations by her parents and teachers and so-called friends about being *depressed* or *on drugs* or whatever . . . what did they know?

Hannah knew it would all be fine on Saturday. Big rave downtown, hot DJ, definitely some X. Everything would be better then, better at the rave. Not that it was the X that would make it all good, though. The X was just the icing on the cake, she thought. Hannah just liked the scene, that's all. It was a good party with good friends. Everyone was so cool to her there—no interrogations, no pretense, just a really good time with really good friends. Everything was perfect at the rave, but everything was awful all the rest of the time.

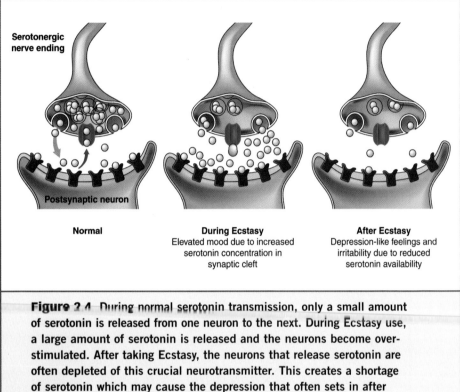

Serotonergic nerve ending

Postsynaptic neuron

| **Normal** | **During Ecstasy**
Elevated mood due to increased serotonin concentration in synaptic cleft | **After Ecstasy**
Depression-like feelings and irritability due to reduced serotonin availability |

Figure 2.4 During normal serotonin transmission, only a small amount of serotonin is released from one neuron to the next. During Ecstasy use, a large amount of serotonin is released and the neurons become over-stimulated. After taking Ecstasy, the neurons that release serotonin are often depleted of this crucial neurotransmitter. This creates a shortage of serotonin which may cause the depression that often sets in after Ecstasy use.

including eating, sleeping, sexual functioning, and temperature regulation; again, these are functions often altered by MDMA use. As one of its most dangerous effects, MDMA's effect on heat regulation may be responsible for many Ecstasy-related deaths.

The Down

Just as the acute increase in serotonin concentration causes a pleasurable state and heightened mood, the "crash" that follows Ecstasy use can also be explained at the biological level. While taking MDMA, serotonin is being released from neurons while reabsorption back into the neurons is blocked (Figure 2.4).

The serotonin eventually drifts away from the synapses and is broken down elsewhere in the brain. This end result is a severe depletion of serotonin in the neurons that need to release it. Therefore, in the hours or days after taking MDMA, the neurons that usually release serotonin cannot perform that task because they do not have enough serotonin to release. The decrease in this important transmitter causes depression by starving the brain of the mood-regulating serotonin.

3

Ecstasy's Long Term Effects

"The high is never the same as the first time, and you are chasing—
you are always trying to do more pills or different kinds to try to get
that same first high, and it does not happen"

—Phillip, former Ecstasy user[4]

LONG-TERM PSYCHOLOGICAL EFFECTS

One of the cruel ironies of Ecstasy use is that, for many users, the first
use of Ecstasy is by far the most pleasurable. That fabulous first
feeling and experience they try to recapture with subsequent uses
never really returns. Many people spend months and even years
trying to chase that first high.

Because of the effect Ecstasy has on the brain's serotonin system,
it may be impossible to ever achieve the same high that accompanies
the first Ecstasy use. Furthermore, beyond the inability to feel that
high, repeated Ecstasy use leads directly to long lasting depression in
many people (refer again to Figure 2.4 on page 24). In fact, a recent
study found that people who used Ecstasy are more likely to develop
depression, and furthermore, the more Ecstasy used, the more
serious the depression.[5]

Another striking characteristic of chronic Ecstasy use is an
impairment of memory. More than 20 independent research groups
have found memory deficits associated with Ecstasy use. These
deficits are directly related to the loss of serotonin neurons that
accompanies chronic Ecstasy use, such that the greater the loss

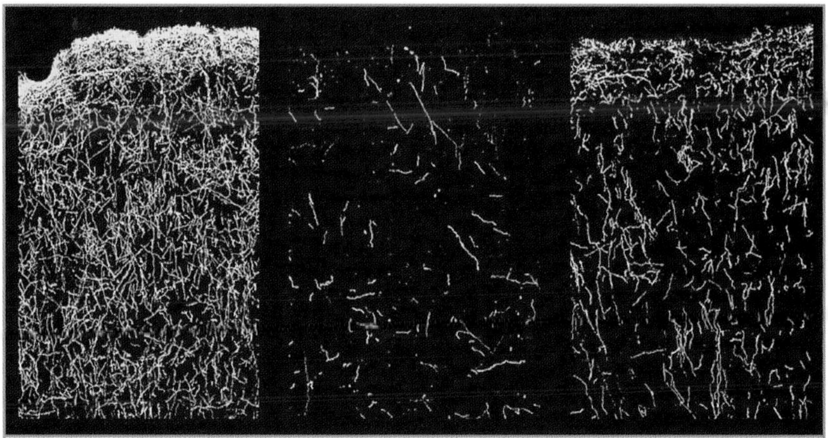

Figure 3.1 This picture shows the presence of serotonin in brain neuron fibers. On the left is a normal, untreated brain. The middle picture shows a similar area of brain tissue, two weeks after Ecstasy treatment. Notice the dramatic loss of serotonin staining. The picture on the right was from a monkey treated seven years earlier with Ecstasy. Serotonin staining is still reduced in these brain sections.

of serotonin neurons, the greater the memory loss. Ecstasy-induced memory loss involves explicit memory; for instance, memorizing a short grocery list or a phone number. When tested clinically on these sorts of memory tasks, people who have used Ecstasy in the past score significantly lower.

LONG-TERM BIOLOGICAL EFFECTS

The most significant long-term biological effect of Ecstasy use in the brain is the prominent and extreme damage caused to serotonin neurons. In 1985, MDMA was first declared illegal largely because of research showing that a similar compound and amphetamine-derivative, MDA, caused brain cell death in animal models (Figure 3.1). Serious and permanent brain damage caused by other addictive drugs like China White (see Box on page 28) led to greater scrutiny of Ecstasy's effect on brain cells.

Because of brain damage caused by a chemically similar drug (MDA), as well as irreversible damage caused by other drugs of abuse (China White), MDMA was categorized as a Schedule I drug by the Drug Enforcement Administration (DEA). The DEA classifies drugs into one of five schedules based on such factors as their potential for abuse and medicinal properties. A Schedule I drug (others include heroin and LSD) is considered highly unsafe, has a high potential for abuse, and has no accepted medicinal value. Thus far, research on MDMA has been clear in showing that Ecstasy is unsafe, addictive, and without obvious medical benefit.

In animal studies, even a single dose of MDMA caused damage to serotonin neurons 12 to 18 months after the dose. This bears repeating; a single dose of MDMA, similar to the amount that most people take in one tablet, kills the cells in your brain that are essential in keeping a person happy. Furthermore, those cells are still dead or damaged a year or more

DRUGS ARE NOT ALWAYS WHAT THEY APPEAR TO BE

In 1982, a group of people in San Francisco began taking a designer drug that was marketed as a "better than heroin" substitute. Physicians began to see a number of young patients with Parkinson's Disease symptoms. By the time they figured out that the common thread was use of this drug, many young people were left either severely paralyzed or even dead. The results were irreversible. The drug, called China White, had a substance in it called MPTP, which is highly neurotoxic to dopamine neurons and brings on the Parkinson's Disease symptoms. This chemical also has properties that make it very similar to MDMA. Very quickly—sometimes within days—young, active people looked like 70- or 80-year-olds with Parkinson's, and, sadly, the effects and paralysis were permanent.

later! Therefore, it is not only those people who repeat Ecstasy use for months or years that may incur neuron damage or death, a single dose is enough to damage and kill neurons. In an even more applicable study, monkeys were given two treatments of MDMA daily for 4 days (a total of 8 doses of Ecstasy). The monkey's brains were then examined either 2 weeks later or *seven years* later. In this study, serotonin neurons showed extremely significant degeneration at 2 weeks after MDMA treatment. While there was some regrowth by 7 years, there was still a significant decrease in healthy serotonin neurons in the MDMA-treated monkeys. This damage occurred in the hippocampus, amygdala, and cerebral cortex, structures responsible for memory, emotional processing, and cognition. These troubling findings probably explain the memory loss due to chronic Ecstasy use. (See note at the end of the chapter.)

Because animal studies provide an incomplete model for looking at the effects of Ecstasy, several researchers have set out to try to determine exactly how MDMA affects the human brain. These recent human studies have shown the same results as previous studies using monkeys; serotonin neurons are just as easily damaged or killed in humans who have taken Ecstasy. Like the animal studies, this loss of neurons in humans is correlated with how much Ecstasy a person has taken and the extent of psychological damage, such as memory loss. In other words, the more ecstasy a person takes, the more serotonin neurons he or she will lose. As more neurons are lost, more psychological damage will occur.

IS ECSTASY ADDICTIVE?

Many rumors exist among teenagers regarding the addictive properties of MDMA. In fact, it is quite common for people to believe that Ecstasy is *not* addictive, a rumor that is perhaps perpetuated by dealers looking to sell Ecstasy. A distinction needs to be made between drugs that cause physical dependence and those that are addictive. Dependence is characterized by a physical withdrawal response when the drug is no longer taken. Drugs like heroin and alcohol, for example, are known to cause physical withdrawal symptoms, such as stomach cramps and nausea when one stops taking the drug. Quitting MDMA does not always result in these symptoms of marked physical withdrawal, so it does not cause the same physical

HANNAH'S STORY:

It was Saturday night and things just were not going well for Hannah. She had driven all the way across town for this rave. There had been one closer to her house, but this one was supposed to be better. There had been this guy at a party last weekend who had said that *this* was really going to be the place to be, the place with all the good stuff. But this was definitely *not* the place to be, she thought. Maybe it was the DJ, maybe the crowd just sucked tonight, but everything was just so dead. There was zero energy in the place. Yeah, people were dancing and there were lights and all, but it just didn't feel good in there. Hannah just didn't feel good in there.

Maybe it was different stuff, she decided, a different kind of X. She had found a guy with some X and had taken it a half hour ago, but it just wasn't doing anything for her. She felt nothing. Her head still hurt even. Maybe it was weak stuff or something. She wasn't sure. All she knew was that here she was, forty-five minutes from home, at the place where all her cares were supposed to disappear, and she just felt nothing— no energy, no love, nothing.

Ugh, she thought, what was wrong with everyone? And what was wrong with that X? Couldn't that guy have scored her some decent X even? Couldn't the DJ play at least *one* decent techno beat? Couldn't at least a few cool people have shown up? Why did the single good thing in her life, her raves, have to go wrong, too?

Hannah found a semi-quiet corner of the room and

dependence that some other drugs do. Some former MDMA users have reported withdrawal symptoms upon quitting, but many do not, and as such MDMA is not characterized as a dependence-causing drug.

Addiction is a different story. Part of the argument depends on how one defines addiction, but several lines of

slouched down against the wall. The floor was disgusting, and the air just reeked of sweat and smoke and bad perfume, but at least she could get away from the crowd for a few minutes. Maybe she'd even bail out, go home, take a few aspirin and go to bed.

"Do I want a what?" Hannah asked. Some random guy had approached her with a little bag full of something, some kind of pills. They were white, kind of looked like X, but they didn't seem like the same stuff she usually got.

"What is it?"

The guy told her it was *better* than X, really good stuff.

"Whatever," she said. "That's just X. And the last stuff I got did nothing for me. What makes this any better?"

He told her to just try it, just give it a shot. He promised this would make her feel like never before. This would make her soar. X was nothing. This was the real deal, he said.

"Alright." Hannah acquiesced.

Ten minutes later, in a pulsing crowd on the dance floor, Hannah wasn't feeling right. She had definitely felt better when she first took this new pill. Her head finally had stopped hurting so much, she finally felt like dancing. But now she was all jittery, sweaty. Things just didn't seem quite right. This was never how she had felt before when taking X. She couldn't even focus—everything was moving around, swirling, dizzying.

"Stand still, will you!" she screamed at everyone around her.

evidence show that Ecstasy is an addictive drug. First of all, one definition of addiction involves craving and seeking a drug despite knowing that it is harmful to your health. Ecstasy fulfills this criterion. A former addict described his life of Ecstasy like this: "It (Ecstasy) may not be physically addicting, but I can tell you I was scared to death of breaking into houses, yet I wanted to get high so badly I was willing to risk it."[6] A recent scientific study demonstrated the potential for abuse and addiction among Ecstasy users; "Continuing to use despite knowledge of physical or psychological harm" was reported by 63 percent of Ecstasy users—a substantial and significant percentage.[7] Another line of evidence demonstrating that Ecstasy is addictive is that animals will continuously press a lever to inject themselves with Ecstasy. Animals will not do that with other non-addictive drugs. In other words, animals will inject themselves repeatedly with cocaine, heroin, or alcohol, but they will not do that with penicillin or even anti-depressants like Prozac.

DOES ECSTASY LEAD TO "HARDER" DRUGS?

Users of Ecstasy often report strong tolerance effects of the drug. Tolerance refers to the occurrence when more and more of a drug is needed to produce the same high feeling. With Ecstasy, it is particularly apparent that users often find decreasing results with each successive use. Ecstasy users are known for always trying to chase that first high and never being able to reach that level again. This fact may be related to the finding that serotonin neurons are being damaged and cannot respond to the drug the same way after repeated usage. In other words, the brain cannot simply produce the same high. As more and more neurons are damaged, it becomes harder and harder for a user's brain to elevate its mood. The cells that caused you to feel so good the first time are literally burned away. Users often try to "boost" the effect then by taking more and more pills ("stacking"). This practice does not work well and usually succeeds only in boosting the stimulant (amphetamine-like) effects, but not the euphoria and well-being effects. The inability to reach that first high also leads many MDMA users to try "harder" drugs, such as cocaine, angel dust, or heroin in search of what Ecstasy can no longer supply. These "harder" drugs, of course, all have their own unique problems, and are extremely addictive and/or dependence-inducing. All of these stacking and alternative drug-seeking behaviors often spin out-of-control and become extremely difficult for teens to deal with. As we will discuss in a future chapter, getting help from an outside source is often the only way to cope with addiction.

Publisher's note:
Recently, one of the central studies showing evidence that Ecstasy can damage brain cells was retracted because methamphetamine, not Ecstasy, was mistakenly used in the studies' trial experiments. Nevertheless, there is still significant evidence that shows the harmful effects of Ecstasy. These deleterious effects include damage to serotonin neurons, problems forming new memories, depression, and heat stroke. More studies must be conducted to provide irrefutable evidence about Ecstasy's specific effects on the brain, however.

4

Other Serious Health Effects

HYPERTHERMIA

One of the most dangerous aspects of MDMA is the fact that it increases heart rate and body temperature and can cause hyperthermia and heatstroke. Through its effects on the hypothalamus, MDMA has direct control over heat regulation in the body and can disable the brain's ability to regulate temperature. The body becomes unable to cool itself, and overheating can quickly set in and cause serious bodily injury. The fact that Ecstasy is so popular in rave settings makes this aspect of its biological effects so dangerous. Raves are hot and crowded, and, because of the stimulant properties of the drug, people using MDMA often dance for hours at a time. Thus, the body's temperature may increase to 105°F or even higher, which can lead to heart failure, kidney failure, seizures, and death. Along with the increasing popularity of the drug, emergency room visits involving MDMA use have skyrocketed in the past 8 years, and the number continues to rise (Figure 4.1).

Because of increased publicity about the dangers of overheating, many Ecstasy users are more conscious about drinking plenty of fluids. While this practice decreases the risk of heat stroke, it can, in rare instances, also lead to problems. Because the liver and kidneys may be overworked, they may not be able to rid the body of all of the fluid that a person is ingesting. If a person is drinking lots of water, but not eliminating fluid by urinating, that can be a very strong sign that something is wrong, and the kidneys may be failing. Without medical attention, this can lead to drowsiness, seizures, and even death.

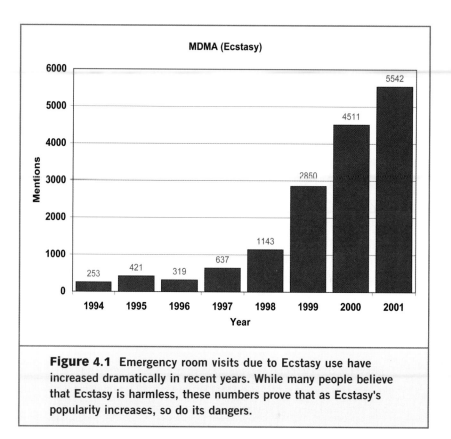

Figure 4.1 Emergency room visits due to Ecstasy use have increased dramatically in recent years. While many people believe that Ecstasy is harmless, these numbers prove that as Ecstasy's popularity increases, so do its dangers.

OVERDOSING AND LACED ECSTASY PILLS

While overdoses are uncommon with pure Ecstasy, they do occur. When someone takes too much Ecstasy, he or she may vomit continuously and vigorously, have fast or difficult breathing, or pass out. People with existing heart, kidney, or liver problems are much more likely to suffer from an overdose when taking Ecstasy.

More common than pure Ecstasy overdoses, it is not unusual to take too much of a "laced" Ecstasy tablet. Pure MDMA tablets are increasingly rare, as suppliers aim to lace the drug with additional chemicals to either increase the high, increase the addictiveness, or just maximize their profit by putting cheaper chemicals in the tablets.

Ecstasy tablets are often laced with other drugs such as LSD, amphetamine, cocaine, methamphetamine, heroin, Gamma hydroxybutyrate (GHB), and Rohypnol® (Roofies). Some tablets are even named according to the drugs they contain. For instance, an "H-Bomb" refers to Ecstasy mixed with heroin. More often than not, the user is not even aware

HANNAH'S STORY:

"This can't be happening. It just can't be happening." Hannah kept repeating this over and over, pacing the halls of the hospital's emergency room. It was as if she were trying to convince *herself* it wasn't happening. But it was.

Hannah had been at a rave that night with a girl she knew from school. She had decided to take the girl out, show her what the rave scene was all about, show her how much fun it was. Hannah still hadn't been feeling as high as the first few times she had raved, but she'd been trying new stuff, new kinds of X. She'd been feeling pretty good lately when she was out. So she thought this girl from school could really use a good time out, too. She was only a freshman. She was doing the girl a favor.

When they arrived at the warehouse where the rave was, Hannah had introduced the girl to a guy she'd met the weekend before. She figured he'd have some good X for the girl to try. Hannah knew she wasn't really into that sort of thing, but then, neither was Hannah the first time she raved.

Hannah's friend had resisted a bit, but she got her to try it finally. After all, she had assured the girl, there was nothing to worry about. Everything's all good on X—especially the first time.

Half an hour later—or maybe it was an hour, Hannah had lost all track of time—the girls had gotten separated, they were immersed in different crowds, dancing, feeling the vibe, that the tablet he or she is taking is not pure Ecstasy. There are several consequences of this, however. First, because the user is often unaware of what he or she is taking, he or she may become very confused, disoriented, and upset when the effect is not as he hoped or planned (for instance, adding amphetamine to Ecstasy may result in a much more anxious, nervous,

---

having a good time. Everything seemed fine. But as Hannah turned around from the people she was dancing with, she saw different lights, red and blue and white, not from the club. They were ambulance lights.

Hannah ran to the exit just in time to see the girl she had brought there being wheeled out on a gurney. They had all kinds of tubes and bags hooked up to her and she wasn't moving. Apparently, Hannah found out, someone had just found her lying on the floor, passed out, and they had called 9-1-1.

When Hannah finally hitched a ride and arrived at the emergency room, no one would tell her anything. What had happened to her friend? Sure, she had tried X, but it was only her first time. And nothing like this had ever happened to Hannah. Something else must have happened to her, Hannah decided. Maybe she got hurt dancing, or maybe she was just sick or something. It couldn't have been the X.

"This just can't be happening."

Hannah tried again and again to convince herself that everything was fine and that it wasn't her fault, wasn't the X's fault. After all, her friend had been totally fine just a few minutes before. One minute she was partying, making friends, the next minute, here she is. Eventually, Hannah learned from a nurse that her friend's body temperature had risen to 106°F. The nurse said she had almost died from overheating.

Hannah just couldn't understand how this happened.

stimulant-like high, while mixing with LSD would produce hallucinations). Second, because the user is unsure how much Ecstasy he or she is taking, he may try to take more to bump up the high, potentially overdosing on either MDMA or one of the spiked chemicals. Cross reactions between drugs of abuse are also common. For instance, alcohol and MDMA both put a serious strain on the liver; taking them together can do permanent damage. Lastly, in the event that hyperthermia or another medical emergency does occur, it is extremely important for a doctor to know what drugs a person has ingested. Because Ecstasy tablets are so often spiked, proper diagnosis and treatment may be impossible, and a misdiagnosis could waste time or suggest treatments that could potentially lead to more serious injury or death.

ACCIDENTAL INGESTION

Another danger of Ecstasy relates to its packaging   that it comes in a tablet. Children often associate tablets with candy or medicine. It is readily imaginable that if a child were to find an Ecstasy tablet (which may be brightly colored, or have a smiley face or a neat shape), he or she might like to eat it. In a well-published account, this precise situation happened to the daughter of movie star Jude Law. While at a children's birthday party at a local restaurant in London, the two-year-old found a tablet on the floor and put it in her mouth before anyone realized what might be happening. Given what researchers know about the potent effects of even a single dose of MDMA, this situation should be very scary for all parents.

HEATSTROKE

Some of the danger signs of heatstroke include: 105°F fever, rapid heartrate, quick shallow breathing, increase or decrease in blood pressure, faintness, confusion, and panic attacks.

Luckily, the tablet was removed before the toddler could eat much of it, and doctors believe that the child was lucky to be unharmed.

HERBAL ECSTASY

In large part due to the popularity of Ecstasy, there has been a boom of so-called "herbal ecstasy" products in recent years. These products are marketed as safe, legal alternatives to Ecstasy, with many of the same benefits. In reality, herbal ecstasy products are not similar to Ecstasy at all. While the dissimilarity may be beneficial in some respects, herbal ecstasy has its own set of problems, worries, and contradictions.

The main ingredient in most herbal ecstasy pills is the stimulant ephedra. While both MDMA and ephedra are stimulants, ephedra has a different effect on the brain's chemistry than MDMA. Ephedra increases blood pressure, heart rate, and gives a sense of energy, but lacks the strong mood-altering effects of ecstasy. Ephedra's stimulant properties have been linked to effects such as dizziness, tremor, alternations in blood pressure or heart rate, headache, and gastrointestinal distress, as well as more serious effects such as chest pain, heart attack, hepatitis, stroke, seizure, psychosis, and death.[8] These problems have been reported in young and older people, even if they had no noticeable health risks. The consequences of taking this drug are so severe that many professional sports organizations have banned the substance (many athletes have used the drug for its weight loss and stimulant properties). These include the N.C.A.A., N.F.L., and International Olympic Committee. The ban was enacted with good reason; several prominent athletes have died while taking ephedra, and investigations persist as to how much of a role the drug played in their deaths. Korey Stringer of the Minnesota Vikings and Steve Belcher of the Baltimore Orioles are two prominent athletes who have died of heatstroke in recent years while using ephedra. The American Medical Association has already recommended a complete ban on ephedra, and although the Food and Drug Administration (which controls the legal aspects of drugs) has not yet made ephedra illegal, it has put out a warning that ephedra poses a significant health risk, and there is widespread pressure for the FDA to make ephedra a controlled substance, so that the importation, manufacture, and distribution of the drug would be under government regulation.[9]

ECSTASY DURING PREGNANCY

Taking drugs while pregnant may cause serious developmental problems for the baby, even for over-the-counter medications. Imagine how much more dangerous a street drug can be, when the dosage, purity, and composition are unknown. Not surprisingly, recent studies have shown that MDMA has serious detrimental effects in a developing fetus. In 2001, a group of researchers at the University of Cincinnati showed

CAN MDMA BE BENEFICIAL?

Some people still believe that MDMA has medicinal value and should not be restricted as a Schedule I drug. In the 1970s, MDMA was used by some psychologists during psychotherapy to allow patients to "open up." Whether MDMA was useful or necessary for this purpose has become irrelevant, however, because of what scientists have since discovered regarding the danger and long-term damage caused by MDMA. No conceivable benefit of taking the drug could outweigh its dramatic toxicity on the serotonin system.

To date, no controlled clinical studies have ever even been proposed to the National Institutes of Health (which funds most research in the USA) suggesting medicinal benefits of MDMA. It is evident that the scientific community does not believe that MDMA has useful medicinal properties.

that when Ecstasy was given to rats during the developmental period corresponding to the third trimester of a human pregnancy, they suffered memory and learning deficits that persisted for the rest of their life. The results were even more disturbing because the dosage used for this study was similar to what people ordinarily take in a single Ecstasy pill.

When the rats reached young adulthood, they were tested on a series of mazes and memory tasks. In one task, for example, a rat had to learn to swim to a hidden platform by first finding it and later remembering where in the pool the platform was hidden. In this task, a normal rat will remember where the hidden platform is located and use it to climb out of the water. By contrast, the Ecstasy-treated rats took much longer to find the hidden platform. Remember, these rats had not been treated with Ecstasy recently, yet they were substantially inferior to their peers who had never been exposed to MDMA. The effects of Ecstasy use during the first two trimesters of pregnancy have not yet been studied. However, hopefully a pregnant woman would choose to not expose her unborn child to this potential risk.

5

Teenage Trends and Attitudes

Ecstasy is no longer a "fringe" drug, confined to upper-middle class suburbanite teens. Though it gained its popularity as a "club drug," seen almost exclusively at raves, Ecstasy now knows no such boundaries. It is in schools, at malls, on the street, and at home. It is no longer even just a teen drug, nor is it a drug reserved for white suburbanites. It stretches to all corners of society, regardless of class, race, age, or sexual orientation. This drug now takes many shapes and forms and is marketed in a myriad of ways.

In the past decade, Ecstasy use has exploded. In fact, although overall illicit drug use by teens markedly *decreased* in the past several years—including use of marijuana, inhalants, hallucinogens, LSD, cocaine, crack, heroin, tranquilizers, alcohol, cigarettes, and smokeless tobacco—Ecstasy use continued to rise, unabated (Figure 5.1).

Finally, however, the tide may be turning. According to recent statistics, between 2000 and 2001, increases in Ecstasy use finally showed signs of slowing. And for the first time since monitoring of Ecstasy use began, Ecstasy use among teens decreased. The hope of educators, law enforcement, and parents is, of course, that their messages on the dangers of Ecstasy use are finally being heard and heeded.

HOW TRENDS AND ATTITUDES ARE MEASURED

Several different agencies and organizations track the prevalence of Ecstasy use in our country. Though Ecstasy has a relatively short

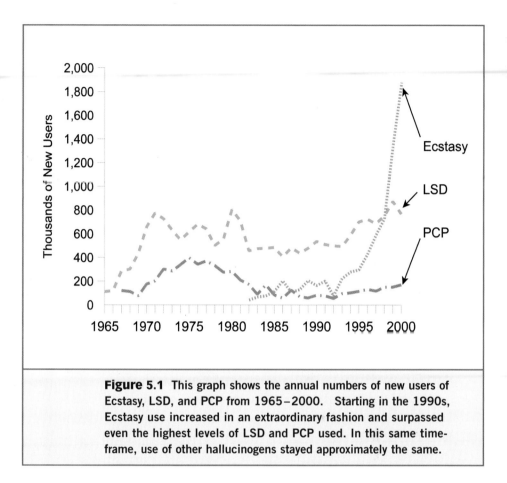

Figure 5.1 This graph shows the annual numbers of new users of Ecstasy, LSD, and PCP from 1965–2000. Starting in the 1990s, Ecstasy use increased in an extraordinary fashion and surpassed even the highest levels of LSD and PCP used. In this same time-frame, use of other hallucinogens stayed approximately the same.

history as a recreational drug in the United States, both government and private agencies have recognized the importance of studying it—particularly among teens.

The primary source of information and statistics on teen Ecstasy use is the United States Department of Health and Human Services (HHS). Each year, they conduct three major surveys and use that statistical data to aid in setting United States national drug policy and also in determining how best to devote financial resources in order to target areas of greatest need. The first, Monitoring the Future (MTF) Survey, is conducted by the University of Michigan's

Institute for Social Research and is funded by the National Institute on Drug Abuse (NIDA). MTF conducts its surveys in schools nationwide and has been tracking 12th graders' illicit drug use and attitudes toward drugs since 1975. Eighth and 10th graders were also added to the survey in 1991. In 2002, MTF collected data from more than 43,000 students in 394 schools across the nation, asking them about lifetime use, past year use, past five month use, and daily use of all types of illicit drugs, including MDMA. For the purpose of interpreting MTF's survey, "lifetime" refers to use at least once during a respondent's lifetime, "past year" refers to at least one use in the year preceding their response to the survey, and "past month" refers to use at least once in the preceding month.

Another United States HHS survey, the Youth Risk Behavior Survey (YRBS), is part of the Centers for Disease Control and Prevention's Youth Risk Behavior Surveillance System, and is also an in-school survey that collects data from students in grades 9–12. YRBS began in 1990 and has been conducted twice-yearly since 1991. The results of the YRBS are difficult to interpret strictly in terms of Ecstasy use, however, because they only ask questions regarding illicit

ECSTASY STATISTICS

- In 2001, over 8 million persons reported using Ecstasy at least once in their lifetime.

- The majority of Ecstasy users are young adults aged 18 to 25.

- Ecstasy users are more likely to have used other types of illicit drugs in the past year than those who did not use Ecstasy.

—Substance Abuse and Mental Health Services Administration

drug use as a whole and do not break it down into specific drugs, such as Ecstasy.

Another important survey conducted by the United States HHS is the National Household Survey on Drug Abuse (NHSDA). This survey is conducted in the homes of teens, rather than in school. Currently, the NHSDA survey is taken via a computer survey for drug-related questions. Though there are some inherent limitations in its methodology, as compared to the MTF survey and others not conducted in-home where teens might be timid to reply truthfully, NHSDA is considered to be a very reliable study and its results highly representative of actual drug use. The NHSDA was conducted periodically from 1971 and annually since 1990.

It is interesting to note that, although the methodologies of these surveys all differ in regard to design, implementation, documentation, and scope, and are therefore impossible to directly compare to one another, their respective results nonetheless do seem to be relatively consistent with each other. Furthermore, the United States HHS has studied the methodology of all of these studies in-depth and has found them all to be of very high quality.

USAGE STATISTICS BY AGE

By examining the results of the National Household Survey on Drug Abuse (NHSDA), it is clear and disturbing that Ecstasy use has risen substantially since the agency began collecting data on MDMA usage in 1992. In fact, the number of current Ecstasy users in 2001 was estimated by NHSDA to be 786,000 (0.3 percent of the population). Initiation of Ecstasy (first time usage) has also spiked. In 1998, an estimated 0.7 million teens tried Ecstasy for the first time. In 1999, that number rose to 1.3 million teens. In 2000, at least 1.9 million teens reported "initiating" Ecstasy. That means that in just two years, the annual number of persons age 12 or older who had tried MDMA rose by 1.2 million.

A separate 2001 NHSDA questionnaire determined that an estimated 8.1 million Americans (3.6 percent of the population) aged 12 and older had tried Ecstasy at least once in their lifetime. In 2000, that number was estimated to be only 6.5 million (2.9 percent). This was a much larger increase in usage for Ecstasy than was seen for illicit drugs in general during the same time period. In other words, while the NHSDA did report an overall rise in illicit drug use during the years 2000 and 2001, there was a much greater proportional increase in Ecstasy use in particular.

The Monitoring the Future (MTF) Survey reveals similarly troubling results for American teens. In the year 2000, they found that, for the fourth year in a row, the number of 8th, 10th, and 12th grade students who used *all* illicit drugs either remained level or decreased; however, MDMA usage *increased* in all age groups. While teens were using fewer drugs overall, Ecstasy use was multiplying. These findings also marked the second consecutive year that MDMA use had increased among 10th and 12th graders and the first year it had increased among 8th graders.

According to MTF statistics, the percentage of 12th grade students who reported using Ecstasy at least once in the past year ("past year" users) rose from 3.6 percent in 1998 to 5.6 percent in 1999 to 8.3 percent in 2000. Among 8th graders, Ecstasy use rose from 1.7 percent in 1999 to 3.1 percent in 2000. Tenth graders' past year Ecstasy use remained statistically unchanged (holding relatively steady at 5.4 percent) during the same time frame, although their "past month" usage increased from 1.8 percent in 1999 to 2.6 percent in 2000. Said NIDA Director Dr. Alan I. Leshner, "This survey provides crucial information on the real-world experience of young people with drugs, and the recent increases in MDMA use are a major concern. Ecstasy is not a 'fun' drug. It is neurotoxic — it severely damages brain cells and has consequences that include dehydration, hypertension, hyperthermia, and heart or kidney failure." [10]

Figure 5.2 represents the percentages of 8th, 10th, and 12th grade students who reported to the MTF survey having used Ecstasy in the years 1999 and 2000. Note that the results are divided not just into year and age categories, but also into male and female categories, and that the percentage is similar for both males and females. For comparison, it is notable that, regarding "past year" usage of illicit drugs in general, it has *decreased* among 8th graders from 22.1 percent in 1997 to 19.5 percent, among 10th graders from 38.5 percent in 1997 to 36.4 percent, and among 12th graders from 42.4 percent to 40.9 percent.

MTF's 2001 survey was notable not because of drastic changes in numbers, but precisely because numbers *did not change* significantly. At last, exploding Ecstasy use steadied and it seemed that perhaps teenage attitudes and trends were shifting, causing MDMA use maybe not to decrease, but to slow at least. "It is encouraging that the trend toward more widespread use of MDMA in 1999 and 2000 appears to have slowed last year," said NIDA Acting Director Dr. Glen Hanson, commenting on the MTF 2001 survey results. "The 2001 survey data also show that greater numbers of high school seniors — nearly half of them, in fact — say they believe there is a great risk in using MDMA. We hope that NIDA's efforts to provide science-based information about the risks of drugs will contribute to further decrease in drug use." [11]

Indeed, although high school teens did report higher rates of "past month" Ecstasy use in 2001 versus 2000, those rates were not as steep increases as in the preceding two years and the increases were not statistically significant. MDMA

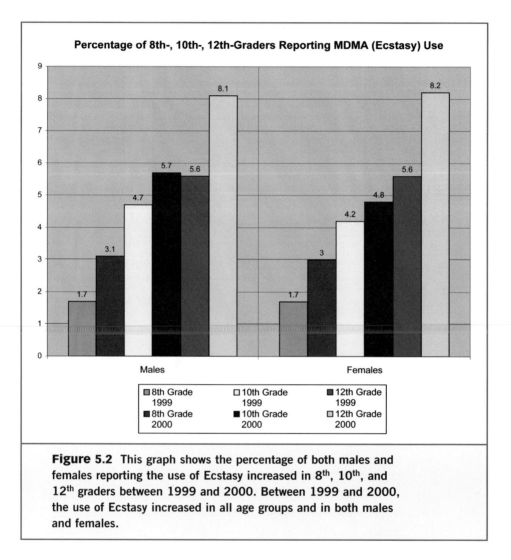

Percentage of 8th-, 10th-, 12th-Graders Reporting MDMA (Ecstasy) Use

Males

Females

| ☐ 8th Grade 1999 | ☐ 10th Grade 1999 | ■ 12th Grade 1999 |
| ■ 8th Grade 2000 | ■ 10th Grade 2000 | ☐ 12th Grade 2000 |

Figure 5.2 This graph shows the percentage of both males and females reporting the use of Ecstasy increased in 8th, 10th, and 12th graders between 1999 and 2000. Between 1999 and 2000, the use of Ecstasy increased in all age groups and in both males and females.

"past month" use in 2001 for 8th graders was reportedly up 1.8 percent, for 10th graders up 2.6 percent, and for 12th graders up 2.8 percent.

The 2002 MTF survey brought even more good news. For the first time since the agency began collecting data on Ecstasy use among teens, Ecstasy use decreased. Overall,

4.9 percent fewer 8th, 10th, and 12th graders were using Ecstasy in 2002 than 2001. The cycle of rising MDMA use appears to be waning.

As an interesting side note, MTF did a follow up study of a group of graduates from each surveyed high school class. In this survey, they found that the number of college students who had used MDMA in the past year rose from 0.9 percent in 1991 to 2.4 percent in 1997. Among young adults, annual Ecstasy use rose from 0.8 percent to 2.1 percent during the same time period. If these statistics follow the same pattern as MTF's other results regarding high school students' usage, it can be inferred that perhaps college student and young adult usage has also slowed and possibly also decreased since this survey was conducted in 1998.

The news regarding Ecstasy use is not all good, however, nor is it all stemming from government studies. In August of 2000, the Psychemedics Corporation issued its own findings regarding Ecstasy use in the United States. [12] Psychemedics is a private corporation and one of the world's leading laboratories for testing hair for the presence of drugs of abuse. The idea of these tests is to have a simple, painless, and quick way to test whether someone has taken an illegal drug of abuse recently. Their results were alarming, particularly when examined in the context of whom they tested and why.

Psychemedics conducted these hair tests almost exclusively at the request of random nationwide employers who had contracted Psychemedics to test potential employees for drug usage. In other words, the tests that Psychemedics conducted were pre-employment drug screenings, presumably issued to persons over the age of 16, and certainly not limited to teens or young adults. Also interesting to note is the fact that these hair tests can detect drug ingestion for the preceding 90 days (unlike urinalysis, which can only detect up to 3 days, and which can be "beaten" by simple short-term abstention).

After 5 weeks of testing, Psychemedics found that when Ecstasy was added to the battery of drugs detected, the number of positives in the methamphetamine category (the category for MDMA) more than doubled. Important to note is the fact that, had the test not been screening for Ecstasy, the results would have been negative in that category. This was unanticipated and highly disturbing news for the government, law enforcement, and parents alike. And it adds weight to the theory that Ecstasy is no longer just a "teen" problem.

WHY TEENS USE OR DO NOT USE ECSTASY

Almost everywhere teens are and want to be, Ecstasy is hard to avoid. Plus, because its desired effects are more or less how teens prefer to feel anyway, it is difficult to determine if they take it for any specific reason. That said, organizations that study teen Ecstasy usage generally look at three attitudinal indicators in order to try and ascertain the "why" behind choosing to take Ecstasy. First, what is the teen's perceived risk of harm in taking the drug? Second, what is the teen's disapproval level of others who take the drug? Third, what is the teen's perceived availability of the drug? These three indicators are essentially the internal pros and cons a person might weigh in making the decision to use Ecstasy.

A high school student's perceived risk of harm in taking Ecstasy is generally formed mostly by popular opinion and gossip and not by current scientific or medical research. That is, students mostly know what they are told, and what they are told about Ecstasy is mostly from their peers. It stands to reason, then, that teens usually hear more positives than negatives about Ecstasy use, simply because their friends may not have all of the facts, and because their friends are much more likely to talk about good experiences than bad ones. Forces among adolescents that help spread the use of a new drug, such as Ecstasy, work much more quickly than the forces that work to contain its use. According to MTF's principal investigator, Dr. Lloyd Johnston, "When a newer drug comes onto the scene, young people hear much more about its supposed benefits than about its potential harms. It can take some time for evidence of the adverse consequences to become known to them."[13] Hence, a teen might decide that, because her friends have had good experiences with Ecstasy, she probably will, too. This could be a decision that she will regret for years to come, however.

Teens generally form very strong opinions of those around them—often quite quickly. Those judgments are also often colored by their circle of friends. Regarding Ecstasy use, for instance, a teen's daily encounters with others who use the drug can weigh rather heavily in his mind when deciding if Ecstasy is right for him. If his close friends use Ecstasy, he is more likely to deem it appropriate behavior. If it is another group of teens who use the drug, people he is not generally approving of anyway, he is likely to view Ecstasy use in a much less favorable light. In this way, a teen forms a basic approval level of those persons who use Ecstasy. Consequently, that same teen essentially makes the decision whether to be lumped in with the Ecstasy users or not. If he generally approves of their behavior, he likely thinks it not so bad— perhaps even good—to use Ecstasy himself. If he generally disapproves of their behavior, he is much less likely to want to use Ecstasy himself.

Availability is a major factor influencing what drugs teens currently favor. After all, the more a drug is out there, the more likely teens are to encounter it, and hence the more likely teens are to actually use it. Marijuana is a key example. In the 1960s, marijuana exploded on the drug scene, appearing everywhere teens were. Eventually, it was not only acceptable in teenage society, it was hip. All it took to begin this revolution was sheer quantity. Marijuana's popularity had relatively little to do with its actual physical effect and more to do with being an easy to get, cheap high. [14] Ecstasy has boomed in much the same way. Like marijuana, Ecstasy is relatively cheap, plentiful, and found in all the right places. Plus, students do not have to hit the streets to score their high. Because its cons have not yet caught up with its pros, it is thought of as relatively benign and therefore is far from taboo with mainstream teens. All students need to do is simply show up at a rave or meet up with someone at the mall and the Ecstasy is right there waiting for them.

Law enforcement and other agencies aiming to control drug production are having a particularly hard time curtailing Ecstasy production, too. Because MDMA is a synthetic drug, composed from chemicals readily available and only loosely monitored by legal chemical manufacturers in some countries (the chemicals are tightly regulated in the United States), Ecstasy labs can easily set up shop almost anywhere and operate undetected with huge profits. There is virtually a constant supply and high availability of MDMA trafficked throughout this country every day.

Studies of teen ecstasy use and perceived risk have shown that as availability increased and disapproval decreased, Ecstasy use went up dramatically. It is also interesting that although teens' perceived risk of using Ecstasy went up in recent years, their usage rates did not abate during those years. Two scenarios are possible: either the calculated risk of using makes the drug even more attractive to teens who, as a rule, enjoy rebelling against the rules of society, or the decline in use is simply lagging slightly behind their fears of using Ecstasy. Given that in 2002, Ecstasy use finally appears to be waning, it is likely that this second explanation is correct— that is, the perceived risk has risen and is finally impacting teen use.

ECSTASY TRENDS

Ecstasy, Adam, XTC, X, roll, hug, beans, love drug, clarity, essence—MDMA goes by many names. It comes in many forms, too. Though usually taken orally in pill form, NIDA's Community Epidemiology Work Group (CEWG) has reported snorting in Atlanta and Chicago, injecting in Atlanta, and anal suppository use in Chicago. CEWG monitors 21 United States metropolitan areas to compile their data. According to CEWG's investigations, Ecstasy is the most prominent stimulant used in Chicago. They also report Ecstasy being sold in many singles bars in Denver and that Ecstasy is the drug of choice among white middle class young adults (age 25+) in Washington, D.C. In Boston, MDMA was the most frequently mentioned drug in emergency calls to the Poison Control Center. In 2001, CEWG also showed clear evidence that MDMA use was spreading from raves and dance parties to high schools, colleges, and other social settings frequented by teens and young adults. Clearly Ecstasy is no longer just seen at raves.[15]

The United States White House's Office of National Drug Control Policy has compiled perhaps the best and most comprehensive information on Ecstasy trends through its *Pulse Check* program. *Pulse Check* monitors drug sales and usage trends via 40 law enforcement and epidemiologic/ ethnographic sources in 20 cities across the nation, selected for their representative diversity. In November, 2002, they released a very detailed report of their findings. They detail patterns and trends according to geography and cover both sales and use of MDMA in the 20 *Pulse Check* cities.[16]

NAMES AND LOGOS

Ecstasy has many names across the country, and often those names evolve from the regional marketing strategies that arise. "Cooks" produce a myriad of shapes and colors of the drug in order to make it more appealing to consumers. Logos, labels, stamps, corporate names, fashion designers, and cartoon characters are often featured on the pills (Table 5.1). Sometimes the slang terms for MDMA are derived from these gimmicks. Of course, some gimmicks are more popular than others in different cities, and fads come and go rapidly.

Pills continue to be sold mainly in loose tablet form. Sometimes sold in small plastic bags, prescription bottles, plastic wrap, coin rolls, or tinfoil, more creative packaging occasionally surfaces. For instance, in St. Louis, large quantities are sold in cigarette packs.

ADDITIVES

Many chemicals can commonly surface in an Ecstasy pill. In Memphis, for example, reported additives include methamphetamine and mescaline, and in Los Angeles, Ecstasy is often laced with dextromethorphan (DXM) or paramethoxyamphetamine (PMA). In Seattle, though, the trend is not lacing MDMA with other substances, but fraudulently *substituting* another drug entirely. In one reported batch, for instance, the confiscated "Ecstasy" pills turned out not to be Ecstasy at all, but rather hormone replacement pills. While certainly causing less harm than Ecstasy, a pill full of estrogen is probably not what many people had in mind when they bought those tablets. Additionally, the estrogen in hormone replacement therapy pills may cause an interaction with birth control pills, decreasing their ability to block pregnancy.

DEALERS

Young adults (age 18–30) are the predominant sellers of Ecstasy on the street. Some cities, however, report Ecstasy sellers as evenly split between young adults and adolescents—Baltimore, Detroit, Honolulu, Los Angeles, Memphis, and St. Louis. Even more alarming, sources in El Paso, New Orleans, and Seattle say that

How Ecstasy is referred to and marketed across 20 U.S. cities

City	Slang terms	Marketing labels, logos, colors, shapes
Boston, Mass.	X, MDMA, adam, essence, flipping, rolling	Logos: bulldog, Calvin Klein, hearts, lightning, McDonalds, Nikes, Playboy, tulips, yin and yang signs, many more
New York, N.Y.	NR	Yes (but names unavailable)
Philadelphia, Pa.	E	None
Portland, Me.	X, E, pure X, roll	NR
Baltimore, Md.	X, E, essence, eve, lovers, speed	None
Columbia, S.C.	E, four-leaf-clover, rolls, S, smurfs	Tablets of all colors Logos: balloons, cartoon characters, diamonds
El Paso, Tex.	E, tachas	Red pill with E
Memphis, Tenn.	X, XTC, adam, beans, clarity, lover's special, rolls, stacks, double stacks, tabs	None
Miami, Fla.	X, E, beans, Mercedes, rolls, roll X	All kinds, change often
New Orleans, La.	X, XTC, pill, tabs	None
Washington, D.C.	X, E, igloo, Mercedes, Pikachu, pills, rolls	Different colors, round shape; E, animals, igloo, Mercedes, Pikachu, pills, rolls
Chicago, Ill.	X, E, rolls	Cartoon stamps Logos: CK (for Calvin Klein), Mitsubishi, Motorola, other corporate names and fashion brand names
Detroit, Mich.	X, E	Logos vary widely
Sioux Falls, S.D.	X, E, roll, snackies (more mescaline based), speedies (more amphetamine based)	Logos: elephants, Mitsubishi, Nike, sun face
St. Louis, Mo.	X, E, XTC, candy, rolls, shamrock, tabs	Proliferation of logos
Billings, Mont.	Peace, serenity, tranquility	None

Source: Office of National Drug Control Policy. *Pulse Check: Trends in Drug Abuse*, November 2002.

Table 5.1 Ecstasy is referred to by many different names. It is also sold using different logos, colors, and shapes. This chart shows how these names and logos are different across the country. Notice that the logos stamped on the tablets are often famous brands, such as McDonalds, Calvin Klein, Nike, Mercedes, and Mitsubishi, or popular cartoon characters such as Pikachu.

adolescents are the primary sellers there. Only Baltimore cites adults over age 30 as the predominant Ecstasy dealers.

Dealers of MDMA are generally independent, except in El Paso, Miami, and Portland, Maine, where both independent and organized sellers have been reported. They are also likely to use Ecstasy themselves. Adolescents, especially, often sell single pills or take the Ecstasy themselves, while adults (25–30 years) typically sell larger quantities and do not use Ecstasy themselves. Ecstasy dealers are not normally involved in other crimes or violence, though.[17] When they are, the crimes are usually drug-assisted rape. Columbia (South Carolina), Denver, Detroit, Honolulu, Los Angeles, Memphis, New Orleans, New York, and Sioux Falls (South Dakota) report this to be true of Ecstasy dealers in their states. Nonviolent crimes such as tagging, vandalism, petty theft, and shoplifting have been reported for dealers in El Paso and St. Louis.

WHERE IS ECSTASY SOLD?

Ecstasy sales take place in central cities, suburbs, and rural areas. While the markets for drugs such as heroin and cocaine are increasingly moving indoors, Ecstasy's market is continually moving outdoors. Beginning indoors at raves and concerts, it moved to other indoor markets like nightclubs, bars, college dorms, parties, private residences, schools, cars, hotels, and the internet. Now, however, it is becoming more and more common to see Ecstasy dealers on the street, at parks, and at other outdoor venues.

Ecstasy sales are usually hand-to-hand exchanges and involve a network of acquaintances or private introductions. How sellers and buyers make contact, though, varies geographically. In Honolulu, Philadelphia, Portland (Maine), Seattle, Souix Falls, and Washington, D.C., sellers approach buyers in-person or vice versa. In Columbia (South Carolina),

Los Angeles, New Orleans, St. Louis, and also Sioux Falls (South Dakota), beepers and cell phones are used to establish connections. Prearranged meetings are often the norm in Chicago and Memphis. Sellers are also, at times, much bolder. For example, in Chicago, hawkers can be seen walking around nightclubs and raves announcing "caps" or "rolls," and Seattle buyers simply ask at the door and are led directly to the source. In Boston, though, Ecstasy is normally acquired before entering the club.

2002 MARKETING TRENDS

- **Columbia, S.C.**—Home-pressed pills no longer seen. No more Mercedes or elephant logos.

- **Seattle, Wash.**—Pills now come in blue and orange (not just white).

- **Miami, Fla.**—Body packing of Ecstasy from Canada has increased. Some smuggling by cruise ship passengers reported.

- **Chicago, Ill.**—Ecstasy being seen on the street for the first time.

- **New York, N.Y.**—Ecstasy continues to spread outside of raves, especially on the streets and in buildings, particularly in The Bronx and Staten Island.

- **Los Angeles, Calif.**—More adolescents are selling than in the past.

- **Philadelphia, Pa.**—Newly organized Russian and Israeli Ecstasy sales groups reported.

- **Washington, D.C.**—Club owners, bartenders, and bouncers increasingly allowing people to sell Ecstasy on their premises.

In some cities, Ecstasy is sold alone. In others, such as Baltimore, Denver, Miami, Portland, Philadelphia, and Washington, D.C., it is sold alongside GHB, ketamine, LSD, marijuana, methamphetamine, powder cocaine, crack, or other pills.

TRENDS IN USERS

Ecstasy users tend to be young adults (18–30), though in some cities (Billings, Mont., Columbia, S.C.; Portland, Ore.; Seattle, Wash.; and Sioux Falls, S.D.) adolescents are believed to be the primary users. Usage is evenly split among genders and is overwhelmingly highest among Whites. There are a few exceptions, however. Hispanics are reported as the primary users in Los Angeles and Miami, Blacks in Baltimore and Washington, D.C., and usage rates are equally distributed among Asians and Whites in Honolulu. In some cities, such as Los Angeles, user groups are defined as the "ravers"

USAGE TRENDS

- **Boston, Mass.**—Ecstasy use increasing among minority high school students and in private schools.

- **Memphis, Tenn.**—Socioeconomic status shifting from high to middle.

- **Sioux Falls, S.D.**—More American Indians using Ecstasy.

- **St. Louis, Mo.**—Growing number of rural residents coming into the city of buy Ecstasy.

- **El Paso, Tex.**—Raves of 200–300 adolescents taking place clandestinely at night on unpoliced, unlit golf courses within the city. Ravers, who can easily disperse, find each other by using laser pointers or putting "glow sticks" around their wrists and necks.

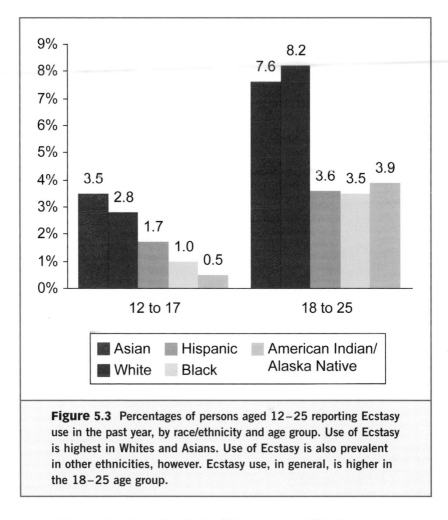

Figure 5.3 Percentages of persons aged 12–25 reporting Ecstasy use in the past year, by race/ethnicity and age group. Use of Ecstasy is highest in Whites and Asians. Use of Ecstasy is also prevalent in other ethnicities, however. Ecstasy use, in general, is higher in the 18–25 age group.

(who tend to be White), the "hip-hop crowd" (who tend to be Black), and the gay circuit partygoers (Figure 5.3).

Although MDMA users are generally from a middle socio-economic background, this varies some by region, and the suburbs are more notorious for Ecstasy use. It is also generally used in groups among friends, but is seen equally in public and private settings (in descending order of reported frequency: raves, private parties, nightclubs or bars, private residences, and college campuses). Some cities report that Ecstasy is often bought but not used in certain settings (high schools and malls).

Users also have specific trends regarding how and with what they consume Ecstasy. Though generally taken orally in pill form, Boston users in their late teens and early twenties sometimes inject MDMA and ketamine intramuscularly, and Sioux Falls users increasingly crush and snort it. Ecstasy is also frequently taken in combination with or sequentially with alcohol, marijuana, or both. Other drugs are also taken with MDMA (LSD, GHB, ketamine, prescription pills, heroin, cough syrup, camphor/menthol inhalants, Viagra®, and nitrous oxide).

HANNAH'S STORY:

Tonight, Hannah is feeling desperate. Nothing seems to make her feel any better lately. X just isn't cutting it anymore. Every part of her body hurts. Every single person she knows either doesn't understand what she's going through or doesn't care. Even all the people she parties with, they care, but they aren't helping. Nothing is.

She decided to come to the rave tonight even though she knows it'll be no good. She just thought she'd give it a try, though. Nowhere else to go. And maybe she'll find something there to get her through the night and have an okay time.

Someone approaches her, tells her to "try this."

"What's this?" she asks. But without even waiting for an answer, "Sure," she says. "Whatever. Just give it to me. I don't care. A pill's a pill, right?"

Hannah swallows it.

Forty-five minutes later, Hannah wakes up somewhere— not the rave—blinded by the glaring white lights overhead. She can barely make out a man's face in front of her. He's saying something to her, but it's all fuzzy and she can't understand him.

CURRENT TREATMENT

Despite increasing Ecstasy-related mortality and emergency room visits, most clients of drug-dependency treatment centers do not report Ecstasy to be a "drug of abuse." Furthermore, only a handful of treatment centers report that their patients use Ecstasy as either a secondary or tertiary drug. Only small percentages of patients in treatment facilities in Seattle, Philadelphia, Baltimore, Miami, and Portland reported abusing Ecstasy. The numbers of Ecstasy users seeking treatment are rising, but are still very small. This is critically important given the known neurological and psychological problems that

"Where am I?" she inquires.

The doctor introduces himself and tells her she has been brought to the emergency room after losing consciousness at the rave.

"Dr. Who? What do you mean?"

He continues to explain that she has had an adverse reaction to a drug she has ingested. He asks her what she remembers last.

"I don't know," she replies. "All I remember is getting really sick. I couldn't stop throwing up. I was just really hot and shaking and . . . "

The doctor tells Hannah that toxicology tests show she ingested MDMA laced with heroin.

"I what? Laced with heroin? That's impossible. All I had was a little X."

After explaining in more detail what has happened to her and that they had to pump her stomach, the doctor goes on to tell Hannah that she had actually stopped breathing for a few minutes. She could have died.

It was just X, she thought. This can't be happening.

Ecstasy can cause. Perhaps contributing to these low numbers is the fact that most treatment facilities serve adults while most Ecstasy users are teens or adolescents. It is clear, therefore, that treatment centers designed to serve teenagers are critically needed to address this problem.

IS EDUCATION WORKING?

> "Teen drug use is once again headed in the right direc-
> tion—down. This [MTF] survey confirms that our drug
> prevention efforts are working and that when we work
> together and push back, the drug problem gets smaller."
>
> —*John P. Walters, director of the White House
> Office of National Drug Control Policy* [18]

MTF's 2002 survey results were very good news for law enforcement agencies, educators, and parents. For the first time since Ecstasy exploded on the American drug scene, its use decreased. Not only were there statistically significant declines in overall usage—after rising rapidly in recent years—usage among 10th graders dipped substantially, and 8th and 12th grade levels showed signs of decline, as well. Past year use for 10th graders dipped from 6.2 percent to 4.9 percent, and past month use went from 2.6 percent down to 1.8 percent.

Perhaps even better news came from the accompanying combination of 2001 and 2002 MTF surveys detailing "perceived risk" and "disapproval" levels. In 2001, 12th graders' perceived risk of harm from taking Ecstasy shot up from 37.9 percent to 45.7 percent. This represented a dramatic and surprising change among teens. In 2002, then, 8th graders' perceived risk from occasional MDMA use increased, as did 10th and 12th graders' perceived risk of trying the drug just once or twice. Also in 2002, teens' disapproval levels in all three grades of others who use MDMA rose substantially. [19]

Together, the apparent leveling of overall Ecstasy use in 2000–2001, the accompanying rise in disapproval rates and perceived risk, and the decline in use from 2001–2002 show that MDMA use appears to be declining, and that decline is likely the result of education. Teens are slowly learning the downside of taking Ecstasy—perhaps because of school programs or anti-drug campaigns or life experience—and fortunately, they are taking that information to heart.

6

Legal Issues and the Fight against MDMA Smugglers

HISTORY OF LAWS SURROUNDING ECSTASY

Ecstasy was largely unknown and unused from the time it was first patented by Merck in 1912 until the 1970s. It was reintroduced in the 1970s by Alexander Shulgin (recall Chapter 1), and soon after, its popularity took off. People even reported being able to buy it in bars.[20] The period of time from 1977 to 1985, when MDMA was still legal has even been termed the "golden age" by those who wish for the drug to be legalized.

In July 1995, the DEA used its authority to temporarily put MDMA into the category of Schedule I drugs, until further hearings could be held. As mentioned in Chapter 3, part of this decision had to do with the fact that a similar compound (MDA) had been shown to produce brain damage in animal models. A year later, in 1996, the DEA officially made MDMA a Schedule I class drug, and as such, access to the drug is severely restricted by the government. While there are groups who have appealed this decision and claim that MDMA has medical value, as of July 2001, there had never been a controlled clinical trial using MDMA, and in fact, the National Institutes of Health (which funds the vast majority of medical research in the United States) has never even received a proposal to study its effect. Dr. Alan Leshner (director of the National Institute on

Drug Abuse) says: "in contrast to what you hear publicly, we at NIH have never received a proposal to study [MDMA] for any clinical indications, which I think is an interesting commentary on the biomedical communities' belief about this substance."[21]

MDMA PRODUCTION AND SMUGGLING

As would be expected given its popularity, the process of smuggling MDMA into America has become an enormous business, and as such, the methods and practice of fighting that smuggling has also become part of everyday life for law enforcement (Figure 6.1). If one just looks at the sheer number of MDMA tablets that are seized by law enforcement authorities each year, it is obvious that the popularity of this drug is growing. In 1993, a mere 196 tablets were seized by the DEA. By 1998 that number grew to over 174,000 tablets. More than 1 million

HANNAH'S STORY:

Sirens and lights never seemed so beautiful. Hannah didn't even mind when Bill, a dealer she'd just met, asked her to hold a bag for him. Why not?

Even the cuffs going on her hands felt good. And fascinating.

Waking up in a jail cell, however . . . that was cold and scary. Hannah cried for hours. Why the hell was she here? The guard said she was being held for possession of a significant quantity of a controlled substance: MDMA. "MD . . . what" thought Hannah. "Ecstasy," he said.

In court, at least, they believed her that the X wasn't hers. She thought that she was off the hook—going home. She was already thinking about scoring some more X that weekend. And giving her friend a piece of her mind for introducing her to Bill. Then the judge said: "Ninety days at the Survivor Clinic."

"Ninety days? That's three freaking months!" Hannah said. Who were they kidding? It was just X. Why do they even care? "I don't hurt anyone. I can do what I want," she thought.

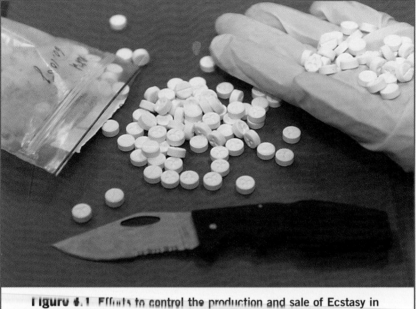

Figure 6.1 Efforts to control the production and sale of Ecstasy in the United States involve many agencies. The Drug Enforcement Agency (DEA), United States Customs, and local police are all involved in seizing illegal Ecstasy tablets. This photo shows a batch of ecstasy tablets confiscated by the United States Customs Agency.

were seized by the DEA in 1999 and more than 3 million in 2000. The U.S. Customs office has shown similar increases in MDMA seizures (Figure 6.2). In 1999, U.S. Customs seized 3.5 million tablets. By 2000 this number had grown to 9.3 million. United States authorities are not alone in this endeavor. During 1999, 14.1 million tablets were seized by Interpol in Europe (Interpol is the International Criminal Police Organization, an international police agency). This number had more than tripled in one year! Global seizures more than quadrupled from 1998–1999.[22] While the numbers of seized pills have greatly increased, it is thought that those numbers represent only a fraction—less than 8 percent—of the total number of pills entering the United States.

It is estimated that approximately 2 million tablets of

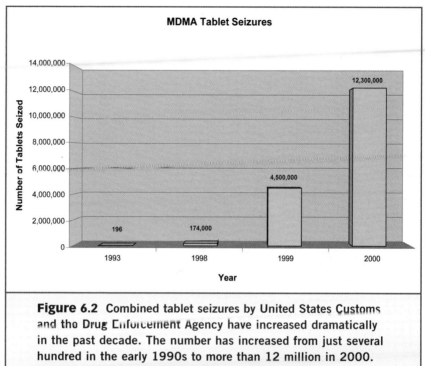

MDMA Tablet Seizures

Figure 6.2 Combined tablet seizures by United States Customs and the Drug Enforcement Agency have increased dramatically in the past decade. The number has increased from just several hundred in the early 1990s to more than 12 million in 2000. This does not include tablets seized in other countries.

MDMA are smuggled into the United States each week.[23] A logical question to ask is: where is the MDMA coming from? The answer is, in large part, Western Europe.[24] The Netherlands and Belgium produce about 80 percent of the MDMA coming into America. One of the main reasons for the concentration in that area is the availability of essential chemicals for the production of MDMA as well as the number of large international commercial airports in the area.[25] Many illegal MDMA laboratories are capable of producing 120,000 tablets of MDMA per day. In fact, one Dutch laboratory was producing close to 400,000 tablets every day. If one tablet costs only fifty cents to make and sells for $25–$50 in the United States, then by the time those tablets are sold, there is a profit of up to 20 million dollars, per day! It is no wonder why the illegal production,

Figure 6.3 In recent years, the United States Customs has cracked down on Ecstasy trafficking. Bags of confiscated Ecstasy, guarded by Customs agents, are shown here. The punishment for trafficking Ecstasy can be quite severe, ranging from 15 months to 10 years, depending on the number of tablets seized. Possession of Ecstasy can also result in jail time, although treatment and counseling is often recommended for Ecstasy users.

trafficking, and sale of MDMA have become such an enormous business by organized crime groups. Despite the popular myths about the beneficial effects of MDMA, money clearly drives Ecstasy production, use, and abuse.

MDMA tablets are often smuggled into the country by couriers who are paid by drug traffickers to smuggle and deliver the tablets (Figure 6.3). These couriers use commercial flights, express mail services, and freight shipments to smuggle MDMA across the border into the United States. While the Netherlands and Belgium are still the key suppliers, other start points for the smuggling rings have emerged, including Spain, the Dominican Republic, and Canada. In the United States, several large cities have emerged as primary drop-off points for drug traffickers. Los Angeles, New York City, and Miami are primary locations, although trafficking is now seen in smaller cities such as Nashville, Tenn., Savannah, Ga., and Montgomery, Al.[26] Couriers who smuggle MDMA into this country have devised many methods to avoid detection. Many have specially designed suitcases that conceal the pills. Pills have also been found smuggled in stuffed animals and baby formula bottles. One of the most disturbing methods of trafficking is when couriers swallow balloons filled with MDMA tablets. The balloons are "recovered" by the couriers after entering the country. It is interesting to speculate on how MDMA use might change if the average rave participant and Ecstasy user knew that their Ecstasy tablet was "recovered" from the feces of a drug trafficker.

LOCAL LABORATORIES

While the vast majority of MDMA is produced in Western Europe and illegally smuggled into America, there are a significant number of MDMA laboratories operating within our

THE COST OF ECSTASY

"At times I robbed houses for television sets and anything else of value. The reason? I needed over $300 a week for Ecstasy."

—Phillip, former Ecstasy addict

"I would ask for money for movies or clothes, then I would spend it on Ecstasy. When that did not work anymore, I would steal money from my parents' wallets."

—Dayna, former Ecstasy addict [27]

borders. It is difficult to produce MDMA in this country because the government regulates some of the chemicals that are required to produce MDMA (such as safrole, isosafrole, and piperonal). The production of Ecstasy requires a series of chemical reactions involving these and other chemicals. Starting in 1990, when the United States government began to regulate these chemicals, the illegal production of MDMA within our borders began to decline. Nonetheless, laboratories do still exist. In 1998 a large laboratory was discovered in Westport, Massachusetts. Another laboratory was found and closed near Los Angeles, as a result of a raid on a mail facility where MDMA was being smuggled into the country. The United States Department of Justice estimates that approximately 12 illegal laboratories are seized each year.[28]

WHAT DRUG MONEY FUNDS

One of the most important issues surrounding drug addiction that ordinarily does not receive much attention is the money trail. It is clear that drugs like MDMA cost very little to make and are sold at a hefty profit. The so-called middlemen, drug traffickers, are often reaping huge profits just by transporting the drug tablets from producer to dealer. Often, those who benefit are linked to terrorist organizations. In 2001, the U.S. State Department released a list of 28 known terrorist organizations. From this list, twelve are known to be involved in drug trafficking.[29] These include: Hizballah, Palestinian Islamic Jihad, Revolutionary Armed Forces of Colombia, Abu Sayyaf Group, and perhaps most importantly, Al-Qaeda. The Taliban regime and Al-Qaeda also received a huge percentage of their operating income through the opium trade (as much as 70 percent of the world's opium trade has in the recent past been produced in Afghanistan). Taking drugs such as MDMA can no longer be seen as only a personal decision. These decisions pay for crime and terrorism.

PUNISHMENT FOR MAKING
AND DISTRIBUTING MDMA

Until the last few years, drug trafficking of MDMA was not punished as severly as many other drugs of abuse. However, the Ecstasy Anti-Proliferation Act of 2000 increased the guideline sentence for the trafficking of 800 MDMA pills by 300 percent, from 15 months to 5 years. The penalty for trafficking 8,000 pills was increased by nearly 200 percent, from 41 months to 10 years.[30] Penalties for sale or possession of MDMA may vary by state, but can be punishable by 3–5 years in prison for a single offense. However, in many jurisdictions "drug courts" have been set up in an attempt to direct drug abusers into treatment and counseling, rather than simply sending addicts to prison. Frequent court dates and court-mandated treatment programs have been extremely successful in aiding addicts in the process of rebuilding their lives.

OTHER LEGAL ISSUES

The legal story associated with Ecstasy does not end with drug producers, traffickers, and dealers. Unfortunately, because of its addictive properties, Ecstasy users must often resort to a life of crime in order to fund their addiction. Story after story exists regarding Ecstasy users who could no longer afford to buy Ecstasy pills and were forced to steal from their family or friends in order to maintain their habit.

7

Treatment and Prevention

"To anyone who thinks Ecstasy is not a serious drug, I give this advice: Stop before you get hurt. I spent years chasing that first magical high and that chase almost killed me."

— Dayna, recovering Ecstasy addict, on her first experience with ecstasy [31]

"Everybody in life gets knocked down at one point or another. The question is whether you get up."

— Joseph Lieberman, Senator of Connecticut [32]

The cost of drug addiction to society is more than most people realize. NIDA estimates the cost at 67 billion dollars per year. Addiction costs include obvious expenses such as treatment and emergency medical care, but also include loss of work time, and police and border patrol costs (see Figures 7.1–7.3). There are also countless personal and psychological costs endured by addicted individuals and their families. In response to these costs, organizations such as NIDA have researched and developed both prevention and treatment strategies for drug abuse and addiction. Because prevention is, in the long run, a much cheaper and simpler alternative than treatment, a lot of research has gone into identifying strategies that work to prevent drug addiction.

PREVENTION
The central facet of many drug prevention strategies is that

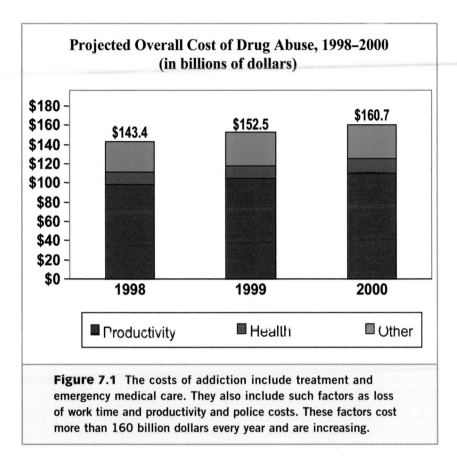

**Projected Overall Cost of Drug Abuse, 1998–2000
(in billions of dollars)**

$180
$160
$140
$120
$100
$80
$60
$40
$20
$0

$143.4 $152.5 $160.7

1998   1999   2000

■ Productivity   ■ Health   ■ Other

Figure 7.1 The costs of addiction include treatment and emergency medical care. They also include such factors as loss of work time and productivity and police costs. These factors cost more than 160 billion dollars every year and are increasing.

education does matter. One of the biggest determinants of whether teenagers use drugs is whether they perceive that the drug is a risk. As Chapter 5 indicated, only in the last year has Ecstasy use started to decline, and that decline corresponds with the fact that the perceived harm of ecstasy is finally increasing to a range where teenagers are realizing that it is a dangerous drug.[33] This point underscores the finding that teaching people (including teenagers) about the scientific findings that show the dangers of drugs like MDMA is a valuable tool in preventing drug abuse. NIDA studies have shown that schools that participate in prevention programs have significantly fewer students who use drugs of abuse. Not only that, but even after the prevention programs ended, students in the schools where the prevention programs were tried continued to maintain a lower usage of drugs of abuse.

NIDA has also identified factors in people's lives that make them more or less likely to use drugs. These have been identified as protective factors versus risk factors. [34]

Protective factors:

- Strong and positive bonds within a prosocial family
- Parental monitoring
- Clear rules of conduct that are consistently enforced within the family
- Involvement of parents in the lives of their children
- Success in school performance
- Strong bonds with other prosocial institutions, such as school and religious organizations
- Adoption of conventional norms about drug use

Risk factors

- Chaotic home environments, particularly in which parents abuse substances or suffer from mental illnesses
- Ineffective parenting, especially with children with difficult temperaments or conduct disorders
- Lack of mutual attachments and nurturing
- Inappropriately shy or aggressive behavior in the classroom
- Failure in school performance
- Poor social coping skills
- Affiliations with deviant peers or peers displaying deviant behaviors
- Perceptions of approval of drug-using behaviors in family, work, school, peer, and community environments

—National Institute on Drug Abuse

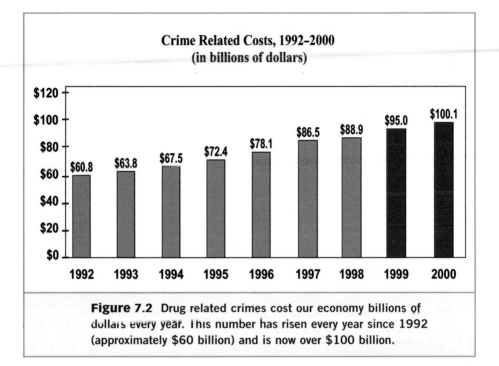

Crime Related Costs, 1992–2000
(in billions of dollars)

Figure 7.2 Drug related crimes cost our economy billions of dollars every year. This number has risen every year since 1992 (approximately $60 billion) and is now over $100 billion.

The hope is that through a combined effort of family, peer, school, and community resources, prevention programs will be omnipresent in the lives of teenagers. Armed with real scientific findings and facts, teenagers are far more likely to resist trying and using drugs of abuse.

TREATMENT

Drug addiction is a disease, and should be thought of as a disease. This is an important point to understand. The good news is that drug addiction is a treatable disease. The bad news is that drugs of abuse, especially drugs such as MDMA, change the brain and are therefore difficult to treat. They actually cause changes in the brain's neurons. Some of the ways in which the brain is changed are known (serotonin neuron loss, for example), however, the brain may also be changed in ways that scientists have not yet discovered. For

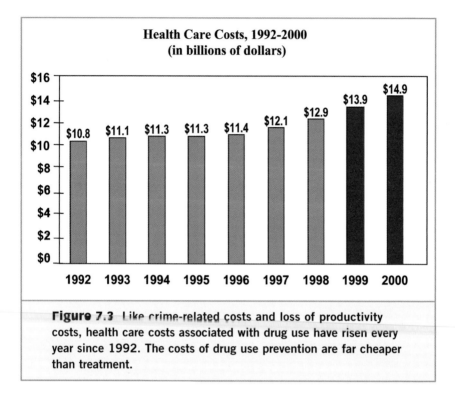

Health Care Costs, 1992-2000
(in billions of dollars)

Figure 7.3 Like crime-related costs and loss of productivity costs, health care costs associated with drug use have risen every year since 1992. The costs of drug use prevention are far cheaper than treatment.

these reasons, treatment of drug addiction is a complicated, individually-tailored process that takes time.

One important aspect to realize about drug addiction is that addiction is a chronic, relapsing disorder. This means that relapse is expected as part of the recovery process. Across all categories of "drugs of abuse," close to 80 percent of people relapse at some point or another. Thus, addressing these setbacks and moving forward is an important step to take when undergoing treatment. While addiction is often popularly categorized as a "lack of willpower," this assessment is not correct, nor is it helpful. The first decision to use a drug may be somewhat correctly categorized that way; however, once drug use has commenced, the brain is altered in such a way that it becomes increasingly difficult to abstain from drug use. Cancer is another chronic, relapsing disorder. Yet when people with cancer have a relapse, the cancer victim is ordinarily not to blame. The same fundamental process should be observed with drug addicts seeking treatment. Relapses will occur; however, that does not mean that treatment has failed. To the contrary, treatment and the healing process must continue.

There are not currently any medications that have been approved for treatment of MDMA addiction. In actuality, very few drugs of abuse have possible medical (pharmaceutical) treatments. Heroin addiction is one disease that is treatable by pharmaceutical means. Heroin addiction is often treated with methadone or levo-alpha-acetyl methadol (LAAM) administration. Similarly, alcohol addiction may be treated with pharmacological tools. However, most stimulants, such as cocaine, amphetamine, and MDMA, do not have medications available for treatment of addiction.

By no means does this imply that treatment is unavailable, though. Behavioral therapies such as counseling, psychotherapy, and support groups are available. Research over the past 25 years has shown conclusively that behavioral treatments do work in terms of keeping people off drugs and reducing criminal behavior. One treatment approach is cognitive behavioral relapse prevention. In this approach, patients are taught to act and think in ways that will help them stay free of drugs. They are taught ways to decline drugs from friends and avoid situations that may be more likely to lead to relapse. Importantly, they are also taught that relapse does not equal failure. Rather, it is a "slip" that can be overcome.

Support groups are also common ways to help oneself in overcoming drug addiction. Many people feel nervous and shy about telling their story to strangers, but knowing that someone else is out there who has experienced many of the same things is often a very helpful and supportive feeling. Also, accepting that you have a problem, and working with others to resolve that problem, is part of the recovery process. Another important aspect of treatment is that it is helpful to know people who have been addicted to a drug, who have quit, relapsed, and kept fighting the addiction. Having a person to talk to, to share with, and to lean on for support is one of the strongest aspects of support groups.

Drug treatment programs are proven to work. In one specific example, a therapeutic approach to treating people arrested for drug-related offenses involved community based care following prison release and reduced the probability of rearrest by 57 percent.

DRUG HOTLINES

There are many places that people who have a problem with drug addiction can go for help. Clinics for treatment of addiction exist in most, if not all, cities. While these clinics are helpful

HANNAH'S STORY!

When Hannah first got to the Survivors Treatment Clinic, it was like prison. She swore that she'd rather die than be at this place with these people. What business did the judge have in sending her here? There were crackheads here, junkies, people who looked like absolute hell. It was insane.

Two and a half months had passed now. It's hard to know exactly when things changed, but somewhere along the line things started to make sense. These people weren't so bad and they weren't that different, either.

Jack was a computer programmer who tried cocaine at a Christmas party two years ago. He used it once or twice a month for awhile. Then, after missing a few weeks of work with a legitimate illness, he was fired. Things really spun out of control. He couldn't tell his wife, so he left each morning as if he were going to work, but instead he'd go get high. Soon, the house was mortgaged, the car was repossessed, and his wife found out—when a dealer showed up at his suburban home. She was devastated. She left him, with their daughter, who cried and screamed "Why are we leaving?" as and very beneficial, many teenagers may be scared to go to a clinic for help, unless forced by a court of law. For these situations, one of the best available options are hotlines that people can call to speak with a counselor about their addiction or problem. Many of these hotlines exist. For example:

- **Drug Help: 1-800-DRUG-HELP**
- **National Drug and Alcohol Treatment Referral Routing Service: 1-800-662-HELP**
- **www.findtreatment.samhsa.gov**

Counselors are trained to listen to the person calling, answer his or her questions, and give advice on what to do. A person will not be required to give his or her name or address. These counselors also will not report anything said to the

she left. It took six more months before he was arrested and sent to the clinic.

Francie was a high school valedictorian. Full ride to the state college. Her first week in college, she tried X. It was eye-opening. She loved it. A year later, her scholarship was revoked when she was arrested for possession. Her parents begged her to stop, but she insisted that she did not have a problem. She didn't even drink alcohol. She could stop anytime. But she didn't. Now all those years of hard work were gone. She was a felon and it hurt.

Hannah saw all of these people and felt unbelievably sorry for them, but also for their families. Jack's wife and daughter, Francie's parents. What did they do to deserve this? She thought about her own parents. She never even talked to them anymore. She hadn't done anything but ignore them or scream at them for months. And yet, they were still there, crying at her sentencing.

Getting them back—getting herself back—that was worth it.

authorities. These hotlines have been set up to help people who need help and to keep them from being too frightened to ask for help.

CONCLUSION

Ecstasy use in America has been increasing greatly in recent years. Fortunately, and because of much hard work, that trend may be starting to reverse course. Information about MDMA and its effects are finally starting to be distributed to those who need it most: teenagers. Some claim that Ecstasy is not harmful. Sound scientific research has shown otherwise.

FIRST PERSON ACCOUNTS OF TREATMENT FOR MDMA ADDICTION

"Over the past 3 months in treatment, I have begun to learn about myself. I have learned to control my emotions and to think before I act. I have learned that I do not need drugs to have fun, to have friends, and to live my life. . . . I feel remorse for what I have done and the damage I've caused to people's property and their lives. Perhaps the first step I can take in making it up to people is by telling you what I have learned. Ecstasy is not a fun, lighthearted drug. It can ruin lives."

—Phillip, former Ecstasy user

"Over the past six months, I have learned to stop living for that next brief high. I have realized that by doing drugs I was going absolutely nowhere and I was throwing my life away. I have focused again on who I am and on my education, something that was always so important to me. I am thankful that my relationship with my family is strong again. My family is now very proud of me and that makes me happy. . . . Life is too precious. Ecstasy is not worth it."

—Dayna, former Ecstasy user[35]

MDMA kills brain cells, and that damage is forever. Some claim that Ecstasy has medicinal value, and should be legalized. Research thus far has not shown this to be the case. To this point, however, no real evidence suggests a valid purpose for MDMA, especially given the harm it is known to cause. Some claim that Ecstasy is a love drug, and that people on Ecstasy do not hurt others, so they should be left alone to do what they want. Former MDMA addicts whose family lives were ruined seeking the Ecstasy high would refute this claim. Furthermore, every cent spent on Ecstasy is funding criminal activity somewhere, and terrorist groups are at the top of that list. At some point, a person has to ask him or herself: Does this drug really deserve to be called Ecstasy?

Bibliography

American Medical Association. "AMA assists in effort to ban ephedra." Accessed at *http://www.ama-assn.org/ama/pub/article/2403-7316.html.*

BBC News. *Ecstasy "link to depression."* Accessed at *http://newsvote.bbc.co.uk/mpapps/pagetools/print/news.bbc.co.uk/1/hi/health/2848489.stm.*

BBC News. *Jude Law daughter in Ecstasy scare.* Accessed at *http://news.bbc.co.uk/1/hi/entertainment/showbiz/2305017.stm.*

Chang, L. et al., "Effect of ecstasy on cerebral blood flow: a coregistered SPECT and MRI study." *Psychiatry Research: Neuroimaging, Section 98:* 2000, 15-28.

Cottler, L.B., S.B. Womack, W.M. Compton, and A. Ben-Abdallah. "Ecstasy abuse and dependence among adolescents and young adults: applicability and reliability of DSM-IV criteria." *Human Psychopharmacology* 16: 2001, 599-606.

Hanson, Glen R. *Testimony Before the Subcommittee on Criminal Justice, Drug Policy and Human Resources , Committee on Government Reform, United States House of Representatives–Research on MDMA.* Accessed at *http://www.drugabuse.gov/Testimony/9-19-02Testimony.html.*

Hatzidimitriou, G, U.D. McCann, and G.A. Ricaurte. "Altered Serotonin Innervation Patterns in the Forebrain of Monkeys Treated with (±)3,4-Methylenedioxymethamphetamine Seven Years Previously: Factors Influencing Abnormal Recovery." *Journal of Neuroscience* 19: 1999, 5096-5107.

Hearing before the Committee on Governmental Affairs. S. Hrg. 107-154. *Ecstasy use rises: what more needs to be done by the government to combat the problem?* United States Senate. One Hundred Seventh Congress, First Session. July 30, 2001.

Hearing before the Subcommittee on Crime of the Committee on the Judiciary. *Threat posed by the illegal importation, trafficking, and use of ecstasy and other "club" drugs.* United States House of Representatives. One Hundred Sixth Congress, Second Session. June 15, 2000. Accessed at *http://commdocs.house.gov/committees/judiciary/hju66177.000/hju66177_0.htm*

Leshner, A.I. "Addiction is a brain disease, and it matters." *Science* 278: 1997, 45-47.

Mehling, R. *Marijuana.* Broomall, Pa. Chelsea House Publishers, 2003.

National Drug Intelligence Center. *Joint Assessment of MDMA Trafficking Trends.* Accessed at *http://www.usdoj.gov/ndic/pubs/642/product.htm.*

National Institute on Drug Abuse. "2002 Monitoring The Future Survey Shows Decrease in Use of Marijuana, Club Drugs, Cigarettes, and Tobacco." Accessed at *http://www.nida.nih.giv/Newsroom/02/NR12-16.html.*

National Institute on Drug Abuse. "Annual Survey Finds Increasing Teen Use of Ecstasy, Steroids." *NIDA NOTES* 16: 2001, 2.

National Institute on Drug Abuse. "Annual Survey Shows Teen Smoking Down, Rise in MDMA Use Slowing." *NIDA NOTES* 16: 2002, 6.

National Institute on Drug Abuse. "Drug addiction treatment methods." *NIDA InfoFacts.* Accessed at *http://www.drugabuse.gov/infofax/treatmeth.html.*

National Institute on Drug Abuse. "Hearing before the Senate Subcommittee on Governmental Affairs." Accessed at *http://www.drugabuse.gov/Testimony/7-30-01Testimony.html.*

National Institute on Drug Abuse. "High School and Youth Trends." *NIDA InfoFacts.* Accessed at *http://www.drugabuse.gov/Infofax/HSYouthtrends.html.*

National Institute on Drug Abuse. "Lessons from preventative research." *NIDA InfoFacts.* Accessed at *http://www.drugabuse.gov/Infofax/lessons.html.*

National Institute on Drug Abuse. "MDMA (Ecstasy)." *NIDA InfoFacts.* Accessed at *http://www.drugabuse.gov/Infofax/ecstasy.html.*

National Institute on Drug Abuse. "Overall Teen Drug Use Stays Level, Use of MDMA and Steroids Increases." *NIDA NOTES* 15: 2000, 1.

National Institute on Drug Abuse. "Studying Comprehensive Drug Abuse Prevention Strategies." *NIDA NOTES* 14: 1999, 5.

National Institute on Drug Abuse. "The Neurobiology of Ecstasy." Accessed at *http://www.drugabuse.gov/pubs/teaching/Teaching4/Teaching.html.*

National Youth Anti-Drug Media Campaign. *Drugs and Terror: Understanding the Link and the Impact on America.* Accessed at *http://www.theantidrug.com/drugs_terror/understanding_impact.html.*

Office of Applied Studies, Substance Abuse and Mental Health Services Administration (SAMHSA). "Ecstasy and Other Hallucinogens." Accessed at *http://www.samhsa.gov/oas/ecstasy.htm.*

Office of Applied Studies, Substance Abuse and Mental Health Services Administration (SAMHSA). "The NHSDA Report." Accessed at *http://www.samhsa.gov/oas/2k3/ecstasy/ecstasy.htm.*

Bibliography

Office of National Drug Control Policy. *Club Drugs.* Accessed at *http://www.whitehousedrugpolicy.gov/drugfact/club/index.html.*

Office of National Drug Control Policy. *MDMA (Ecstasy) Fact Sheet.* Accessed at *http://www.whitehousedrugpolicy.gov/publications/pdf/ncj188745.pdf.*

Office of National Drug Control Policy. *Pulse Check: Trends in Drug Abuse.* Accessed at *http://www.whitehousedrugpolicy.gov/publications/drugfact/pulsechk/nov02/ecstasy.html.*

Psychemedics Corporation. "Media Reports Indicate Ecstasy Use Growing: New Hair Analysis Tests Demonstrate To What Degree." Accessed at *http://www.preemploymentdrugtests.com/ecstasy_drugtest_results.htm.*

Saunders, Nicholas. *E is for Ecstasy.* London, UK: Nicholas Saunders, 1994.

United States Food and Drug Administration. "Adverse Events with Ephedra and Other Botanical Dietary Supplements." FDA Medical Bulletin. Accessed at *http://vm.cfsan.fda.gov/~dms/ds-ephe2.html.*

References

1. Hearing before the Committee on Governmental Affairs. S. Hrg. 107-154. *Ecstasy use rises: what more needs to be done by the government to combat the problem?* United States Senate. One Hundred Seventh Congress, First Session. July 30, 2001.

2. Ibid.

3. Leshner, A.I. "Addiction is a brain disease, and it matters." *Science* 278: 45-47, 1997.

4. Hearing before the Committee on Governmental Affairs. Op. cit.

5. BBC News. *Ecstasy "link to depression."* Accessed at http://newsvote.bbc.co.uk/mpapps/pagetools/print/news.bbc.co.uk/1/hi/health/2848489.stm.

6. Hearing before the Committee on Governmental Affairs. Op.cit.

7. BBC News. Op. cit.

8. National Drug Intelligence Center. *Joint Assessment of MDMA Trafficking Trends.* Accessed at http://www.usdoj.gov/ndic/pubs/642/product.htm.

9. American Medical Association. "AMA assists in effort to ban ephedra." Accessed at http://www.ama-assn.org/ama/pub/article/2403-7316.html.

10. National Institute on Drug Abuse. "Annual Survey Finds Increasing Teen Use of Ecstasy, Steroids." *NIDA NOTES* 16: 2001, 2.

11. National Institute on Drug Abuse. "Annual Survey Shows Teen Smoking Down, Rise in MDMA Use Slowing." *NIDA NOTES* 16: 2002, 6.

12. Psychemedics Corporation. "Media Reports Indicate Ecstasy Use Growing: New Hair Analysis Tests Demonstrate To What Degree." Accessed at http://www.preemploymentdrugtests.com/ecstasy_drugtest_results.htm.

13. National Institute on Drug Abuse. "Overall Teen Drug Use Stays Level, Use of MDMA and Steroids Increases." *NIDA NOTES* 15: 2002, 1.

14. R. Mehling. *Marijuana.* Broomall, Pa. Chelsea House Publishers, 2003.

15. National Institute on Drug Abuse. "MDMA (Ecstasy)." *NIDA InfoFacts.* Accessed at http://www.drugabuse.gov/Infofax/ecstasy.html.

16. Office of National Drug Control Policy. "Pulse Check: Trends in Drug Abuse." Accessed at http://www.whitehousedrugpolicy.gov/publications/drugfact/pulsechk/nov02/ecstasy.html.

17. Ibid.

18. National Institute on Drug Abuse. "2002 Monitoring the Future Survey Shows Decrease in Use of Marijuana, Club Drugs, Cigarettes, and Tobacco." Accessed at http://www.nida.nih.giv/Newsroom/02/NR12-16.html.

References

19. National Institute on Drug Abuse. "High School and Youth Trends." *NIDA InfoFacts*. Accessed at http://www.drugabuse.gov/Infofax/HSYouthtrends.html.

20. Nicholas Saunders. *E is for Ecstasy*. London, UK: Nicholas Saunders, 1994.

21. Hearing before the Committee on Governmental Affairs. Op.cit.

22. Office of National Drug Control Policy. *MDMA (Ecstasy) Fact Sheet*. Accessed at http://www.whitehousedrugpolicy.gov/publications/pdf/ncj188745.pdf.

23. Hearing before the Subcommittee on Crime of the Committee on the Judiciary. *Threat posed by the illegal importation, trafficking, and use of ecstasy and other "club" drugs*. United States House of Representatives. One Hundred Sixth Congress, Second Session. June 15, 2000. Accessed at http://commdocs.house.gov/committees/judiciary/hju66177.000/hju66177_0.htm.

24. Hearing before the Committee on Governmental Affairs, op.cit.

25. Office of National Drug Control Policy. Op cit.

26. Hearing before the Subcommittee on Crime of the Committee on the Judiciary. Op cit.

27. Hearing before the Committee on Governmental Affairs. Op.cit.

28. National Drug Intelligence Center. Op cit.

29. National Youth Anti-Drug Media Campaign. *Drugs and Terror: Understanding the Link and the Impact on America*. Accessed at http://www.theantidrug.com/drugs_terror/understanding_impact.html.

30. Office of National Drug Control Policy. *Club Drugs*. Accessed at http://www.whitehousedrugpolicy.gov/drugfact/club/index.html.

31. Hearing before the Committee on Governmental Affairs. Op.cit.

32. Ibid.

33. National Institute on Drug Abuse. Op cit.

34. Ibid.

35. Hearing before the Committee on Governmental Affairs. Op. cit.

Further Reading

Kuhn, Cynthia, Jeremy Foster, and Leigh Wilson. *Buzzed: The Straight Dope About the Most Used and Abused Drugs from Alcohol to Ecstasy.* New York: W.W. Norton and Company, 1998.

Dupont, Robert, and Betty Ford. *The Selfish Brain: Learning from Addiction.* Center City, Minn.: Hazelden Information Education, 2000.

Leshner, A.I. "Addiction is a brain disease, and it matters." *Science* 278: 1997 45-47.

Peroutka, Stephen (ed.). "Ecstasy: The Clinical, Pharmacological, and Neurotoxicological Effects of the Drug MDMA." *Topics in the Neurosciences.* Vol. 9. Boston: Kluwer Academic Publishers, 1989.

Websites

Drug Enforcement Agency (DEA)
www.usdoj.gov/dea

National Clearinghouse for Alcohol and Drug Information (NCADI)
http://www.health.org

National Household Survey on Drug Abuse
www.samhsa.gov/oas/nhsda.htm

National Institute on Drug Abuse
www.drugabuse.gov

National Institute on Drug Abuse's Club Drugs Website
www.clubdrugs.org

National Library of Medicine Club Drugs Webpage
www.nlm.nih.gov/medlineplus/clubdrugs.html

National Youth Anti-Drug Media Campaign
www.theantidrug.com

Partnership for a Drug-Free America
http://drugfreeamerica.com

PBS show "In the Mix"
www.pbs.org/inthemix/ecstasy_index.html

Index

Index

Index

Index

Picture Credits

About the Author

Brock Schroeder earned a Bachelor's degree in biology at Washington University in Saint Louis and a Ph.D. in Neuroscience at the University of Wisconsin–Madison. His research, focusing on the neuroscience of drug addiction, has been published in academic journals such as *Synapse, Neuroscience, Neuropsychopharmacology,* and *Behavioral Neuroscience.* He also has spent a great deal of time working to bring scientific research findings into elementary and high school classrooms, and received a National Science Foundation fellowship to develop a web-based substance abuse curriculum. Currently, Dr. Schroeder is a post-doctoral fellow at the University of California–San Diego, where he has changed his research focus and is investigating the cellular basis of Alzheimer's Disease.

About the Editor

David J. Triggle is a University Professor and a Distinguished Professor in the School of Pharmacy and Pharmaceutical Sciences at the State University of New York at Buffalo. He studied in the United Kingdom and earned his B.Sc. degree in chemistry from the University of Southampton and a Ph.D. degree in chemistry at the University of Hull. Following post-doctoral work at the University of Ottawa in Canada and the University of London in the United Kingdom, he assumed a position at the School of Pharmacy at Buffalo. He served as Chairman of the Department of Biochemical Pharmacology from 1971 to 1985 and as Dean of the School of Pharmacy from 1985 to 1995. From 1995 to 2001 he served as the Dean of the Graduate School, and as the University Provost from 2000 to 2001. He is the author of several books dealing with the chemical pharmacology of the autonomic nervous system and drug-receptor interactions, some four hundred scientific publications, and has delivered over one thousand lectures worldwide on his research.